**"Well, I'm here i̶̶̶̶̶̶̶̶̶̶̶̶̶̶̶̶̶̶̶̶̶ saw your sign. I'̶̶̶̶̶̶̶̶̶̶̶̶̶̶̶̶̶̶̶̶̶̶̶ wondered if by chance your Dr. J. Beaumont is the same person I went to college with. Dr. Jonah Beaumont?"**

Unable to restrain his curiosity a moment more, Jonah took the two steps necessary to get to the front desk.

Their eyes met, and Jonah's heart did a weird little stutter-step, before starting to pound way harder than was appropriate for the moment.

Neither of them spoke for the space of a couple of seconds, although it somehow seemed to stretch on for an eternity, during which time Jonah took in the face staring back at him.

It was sharp, almost vulpine. Ruddy, with high cheekbones, a narrow nose that flared slightly at the end and a cheeky, full-lipped smile. His thick, dark hair fell to his shoulders and could have seemed effeminate except that the man himself exuded masculinity and sex appeal.

But it was the eyes that brought back the sharpest memories. Light brown, almost coppery, and gleaming with good humor. Jonah remembered wanting to see them turn his way, again and again, although even when they did it was never in the way he wanted them to.

Dear Reader,

I'm always looking for silver linings. It's a product both of my upbringing and of my ongoing mental health challenges. One of those silver linings has been the support of my village: family, friends and the editors at Harlequin. It's allowed me to continue writing even when I felt I had nothing left to say nor the ability to put the words on the page. It's been a hard road, and I'm still climbing the hill, but one of the things I've learned is the fallacy of believing that if I can just get to some mythical point, everything will be perfect.

My heroes, Rob and Jonah, haven't learned that lesson yet. Both have dreams that have somehow turned into obsessions, and unfortunately those dreams are completely at odds. One craves adventure, the other stability, and neither of them is prepared to fall in love and have to question everything they've worked toward. Yet, in life, the only constant is change, and the only real question is how hard you're willing to fight to keep the status quo!

Thank you for reading *Celebrity Vet's Second Chance*, and I hope you fall in love with Rob and Jonah the way I have.

One love,

*Ann McIntosh*

# CELEBRITY VET'S
# SECOND CHANCE

**ANN McINTOSH**

MEDICAL ROMANCE

**Harlequin®**
# MEDICAL
# ROMANCE

Recycling programs for this product may not exist in your area.

ISBN-13: 978-1-335-94294-4

Celebrity Vet's Second Chance

Harlequin Enterprises ULC
22 Adelaide St. West, 41st Floor
Toronto, Ontario M5H 4E3, Canada
www.Harlequin.com

**Printed in U.S.A.**

**Ann McIntosh** was born in the tropics, lived in the frozen north for a number of years and now resides in sunny central Florida with her husband. She's a proud mama to three grown children, loves tea, crafting, animals (except reptiles!), bacon and the ocean. She believes in the power of romance to heal, inspire and provide hope in our complex world.

### Books by Ann McIntosh

### Harlequin Medical Romance

### *Carey Cove Midwives*

*Christmas Miracle on Their Doorstep*

### *Boston Christmas Miracles*

*The Nurse's Holiday Swap*

*Christmas with Her Lost-and-Found Lover*
*Night Shifts with the Miami Doc*
*Island Fling with the Surgeon*
*Christmas Miracle in Jamaica*
*How to Heal the Surgeon's Heart*
*One-Night Fling in Positano*
*Twin Babies to Reunite Them*
*The Vet's Caribbean Fling*

Visit the Author Profile page at Harlequin.com.

For my partners in crime, Traci Douglass and
Amy Ruttan. Thanks for keeping me somewhat sane!

**Praise for
Ann McIntosh**

"I found Ann McIntosh's *Christmas with Her
Lost-and-Found Lover* to be an exciting, entertaining
and adorable read. I really, really enjoyed it and would
recommend it to anyone who loves their heroines
motivated and smart and their heroes loving and
genuine. Wonderful read!"

—*Harlequin Junkie*

# CHAPTER ONE

DR. JONAH BEAUMONT blinked against the grittiness in his eyes, his body aching as though he'd already worked for eight hours, although it was only nine thirty in the morning.

Besides the clinic being short-staffed and extra busy, getting out of bed to tend to a sick patient only to have the animal die on you was always a draining experience.

At least, it was for him.

Pushing the memory aside, he finished bandaging the irate duck's foot and, over the angry squawks of Jennifer Mulligan's pet mallard Hofstetter, said, "You're gonna have to isolate this baby, keep him confined and out of the water till the wound heals. Bumblefoot can become serious if it doesn't completely heal."

"He won't like that," Jennifer replied, struggling to hold the wriggling Hofstetter still. "He's used to being in charge of the flock. There'll be a mighty fuss going on all day, with him trying to boss them around from in the pen."

Jonah chuckled. "I feel for you, especially when it comes time to rebandage this foot. He doesn't much like this part of the proceedings, any more than he liked me cutting out the abscess."

Jennifer snorted. "I'll get Fen to hold him while I do it. She's the only one he'll allow to do whatever she likes with him."

Jonah straightened and peeled off his gloves. "That little girl of yours is a natural with the animals. I've never seen anything like it."

"She's already decided she wants to be a vet when she grows up," Jennifer said, shaking her head as she maneuvered the still squawking Hofstetter into a pet carrier. "Bruce and I are trying to figure out how to afford it."

"Tell her she needs to keep her nose to the grindstone at school, and when she's a little older, as long as I'm still around, she can come here as an intern after school and on the weekends. That'll go a long way toward helping her get scholarships and grants."

Jennifer's smile lit up her face and made the exhaustion weighing on Jonah lift a little.

"I'll tell her," Jennifer said. Then her smile faded. "I heard about Marnie Rutherford's mare dying this morning. What a blow that must have been to her." She hesitated a beat, then added, "And to you."

And, just like that, the weight of the world seemed to drop back onto his shoulders and, with it, that pervasive sense that no matter how hard he tried, he could never do or be enough.

"Yeah," he replied, turning away to toss the gloves into the garbage. He used the excuse of grabbing a wet wipe to keep his back to Jennifer. "She was devastated. Unfortunately, there was nothing I could do."

Behind him, he heard Jennifer pick up the carrier, and he turned to face her once more, knowing his expression wouldn't betray his real feelings. He'd had years to perfect hiding them, since his clients needed to have complete confidence in his abilities, even when he didn't.

"Torsion is like that a lot, isn't it? Quick to come on, and quick to kill."

Jennifer spoke matter-of-factly—a farmer to the core, who understood all too well the vagaries of animal husbandry. Jonah was opening the door for her and pondering how to respond to her statement when the waiting room suddenly erupted in a cacophony of barks, shouts, squeals and bleats.

With a muttered, "Excuse me," Jonah slipped

past Jennifer in the corridor and ran toward the door leading to the waiting area. Throwing it open, he was in time to see a tall, dark-haired stranger put Geoffry the billy goat into a professional-looking horn hold, while his owner, old Mrs. Kimball, fluttered around ineffectually. Geoffry, not being used to such masterful treatment, seemed too shocked to do anything but stay still.

Something about the back view of the man holding the goat sparked a rush of awareness in Jonah, but he wasn't sure whether it was familiarity or something completely different. Instinct had him turn his attention, instead, to the rest of the people in the waiting room, most of whom were hanging on to their upset and anxious pets for dear life. Yet, there was also excitement on more than one face, and there'd been a smattering of applause too.

"Oh, Geoffry." Samantha, one of the vet techs, brushed past Jonah in the doorway and crossed the room to take the goat's harness. "Mrs. Kimball, we always ask you to leave Geoffry outside until it's time for Dr. Beaumont to see him. He's such a spicy guy. And he doesn't like dogs."

"That's not true," Mrs. Kimball replied. "He gets on fine with Mic and Mac at home. I'm sure that doggy must have growled at him."

Considering the dog in question had somehow wedged itself under its owner's chair despite being at least a hundred pounds, Jonah somehow doubted that statement.

The German shepherd mix looked frankly terrified.

Samantha couldn't get through the door with him standing there, so Jonah stepped back to let them pass as the goat wrangler walked away from him toward the reception desk. There was a brief shuffling of people—Sam, Geoffry and Mrs. Kimball going into the corridor, the patient Jennifer with her carrier leaving—and then the door swung shut, leaving Jonah still standing there, a little breathless and somehow confused.

*Must be the lack of sleep.*

But rather than go back to the examination room to see his next patient, he found himself circling over to behind the reception desk, wanting to see the strange man's face.

Hear his voice.

"Hi," the receptionist, Laura, said, while Jonah hung back out of sight behind the dividing wall, waiting to hear their interaction. She was fairly new, so if Jonah was caught spying on her, he could legitimately say he was evaluating her skills with the clients. "Thanks so much for jumping in like that. We really appreciate it."

"No problem," the man replied, amusement clear in his tone. The hair on Jonah's arms and back of his neck lifted, leaving a tingling sensation behind that made him shiver. "That poor dog didn't know what to do with itself, and the goat clearly runs the show, wherever he is."

Laura giggled, and someone else nearby called out, "You got it, man. Geoffry's a beast."

"So, what can we do for you today?" Laura asked.

"Well, I'm here in town on business, and saw your sign. I'm a vet too, and wondered if by chance your Dr. J. Beaumont is the same person I went to college with. Dr. Jonah Beaumont?"

Unable to restrain his curiosity a moment more, Jonah took the two steps necessary to get to the front desk and stood behind Laura, drawing the attention of the man standing in front of her.

Their eyes met, and Jonah's heart did a weird little stutter step before starting to pound way harder than was appropriate for the moment.

Neither of them spoke for the space of a couple of seconds, although it somehow seemed to stretch on for an eternity, during which time Jonah took in the man in front of him.

His first thought was, *expensive*.

It wasn't often you saw someone dressed that

way in small-town Butler's Run. Although not much of a clotheshorse himself, Jonah knew enough to ascertain that the casual outfit—which fit to perfection—hadn't been bought in a chain store. The leather jacket alone probably cost more than all the clothes in his closet at home. And while it was paired with jeans and a flannel shirt, he'd bet both garments had designer labels in them as well.

All this he took in with a sweeping glance, down then up, just as aviator sunglasses were being lifted to reveal the other man's face.

It was sharp, almost vulpine. Ruddy, with high cheekbones, a narrow nose that flared slightly at the end, and a cheeky, full-lipped smile. His thick dark hair fell to his shoulders and could have seemed effeminate except that the man himself exuded masculinity and sex appeal.

The consummate Latin lover come to life, with a dash of what looked like Hollywood flair added in.

But it was the eyes that brought back the sharpest memories. Light brown, almost coppery, and gleaming with good humor. Jonah remembered wanting to see them turn his way, again and again, although even when they did it was never in the way he wanted them to.

Jonah forcibly squashed that thought, and the rush of arousal that came with it.

Instead, he forced himself to remember how nice and kind the man across the desk had been to him. And also, that he'd always been so far out of Jonah's league it sometimes felt impossible they existed in the same universe, much less the same world.

"I can't believe it." Jonah finally found his voice and was amazed when it sounded fairly normal, although there was a definite edge of surprise—or shock—to it. "Rob Sandoval? What the heck are you doing here in Butler's Run?"

Rob couldn't help grinning across the reception desk at Jonah Beaumont, who looked almost the same as he had ten years before, which was the last time they'd seen each other.

About three inches shorter than Rob's six feet one inch, Jonah was broad-shouldered and barrel-chested, stocky but obviously still muscular. His scrub top hung down over a taut belly and clung to bulging biceps. There was definitely a touch of silver in his short black hair, and a few more creases in his chocolate-dark skin, especially at the corners of his mouth and eyes. But that full-lipped mouth still smiled in the same restrained way, and the deep-set eyes, with their heavy lids, gave his face a sleepy, sexy look, in contrast to what Rob remembered as a sharp intellect.

Behind him he could hear the murmuring of the people in the waiting room, and the receptionist was looking from him to the card he'd handed her, back and forth, as though trying to figure something out.

It made him grin a little wider.

Small towns, no matter where in the world they were, were all the same. Almost everybody knew everybody else's business, and what they didn't know, they'd nose out or make up.

He'd had enough experience since starting the video shorts and documentaries to realize someone would recognize him when he'd walked into the clinic. Even in the most remote corners of the States, at least one person had known about his alter ego, Vet Vic, who traveled around revealing the secret lives of animals.

Clearly there were a few Vet Vic fans in the waiting area, and they were probably waiting for him to admit to who he was.

But, instead of answering Jonah's question about why he was there, Rob couldn't resist leaving them all hanging, just a little.

"Why would you say it like that, as though

Butler's Run was in the middle of the Kalahari or something?"

Jonah's lips twisted slightly, the surprise fading to be replaced by rueful amusement.

Or was it annoyance?

"It might as well be. Butler's Run, South Carolina, isn't on the beaten path like, say, New York City, is it?"

"Thank the good Lord for that," drawled one of the clients, bringing a wave of laughter and murmurs of agreement.

"True," Rob replied, then glanced over his shoulder at the crowded waiting area. "Listen, I can see you're busy. I'll be here for a few weeks. Want to get some lunch and catch up?"

Jonah rubbed the back of his neck as he nodded. "Sure. I'd love to catch up. And normally lunch would be good, but we're short-staffed today, and I might end up working through it."

"Why not ask Vet Vic to help you out?" called someone from behind him, making Rob mentally shake his head. "If he's not filming today."

Whoever it was obviously just couldn't take the suspense anymore.

"Vet Vic?" Jonah's forehead creased with obvious confusion. "Filming?"

"I knew it!" The receptionist bounced in her

seat. "I've watched all your videos. They're great."

"Where you been, Doc? Didn't you hear they were coming to do a piece on the Marsh Tacky?"

"Haven't you seen any of this guy's documentaries?"

"Vet Vic is the bomb."

Rob held up his hand, cutting through the overlapping chatter and hubbub. While there was a dawning of understanding in Jonah's expression, the tumult couldn't be allowed to continue. Turning so he could see the waiting room, he scanned it, making eye contact with most of the clients there.

"Come on, guys. Give Doc Beaumont a break, will you? He can't just have some strange vet come in and start working on his patients. There are liability issues."

"Oh, forget about all that legal claptrap," a woman with pink hair said. "Anyone here gonna sue if something happens?"

The resulting negative response was seemingly universal, but Rob shook his head.

"I'm not putting Jonah in that position."

"He's got interns and stuff working for him all the time. How would it be any different?"

Clearly the pink-haired lady was determined not to give up without a fight, and Rob hoped there were no emergencies in the back, waiting for Jonah's attention. The entire situation was getting completely out of hand. The best thing he could do was leave, before it went any further.

And when he turned back to the desk to apologize and tell Jonah goodbye, there was that expression again—the one he couldn't decide was amusement or irritation. But, to his surprise, before he could speak, Jonah's face smoothed of all emotion, and he said, "If you're free, I really could use an extra pair of hands today. I have two vet techs and my intern out sick."

Rob searched the other man's face, trying to figure out if he was just pandering to the clients' demands, but there was no reading him.

He hesitated for a moment, not wanting to cause a disruption to the running of the clinic. And yet, the opportunity was too good to pass up.

"You're sure?" he asked, and got a nod in return. "Well, then, can you lend me some scrubs?"

A ridiculous cheer went up from the waiting clients, and Rob glimpsed Jonah's mouth twist again as he turned away from the desk.

# CHAPTER TWO

THE ENTIRE SITUATION felt completely surreal to Jonah, and, as he went to open the door to let Rob into the surgery area, he vaguely wondered if he'd fallen asleep and was dreaming.

He'd heard about the documentary featuring the Carolina Marsh Tacky equine breed and "Vet Vic," the celebrity veterinarian set to star in it, but hadn't really paid much attention. Never in a million years would he have thought Vet Vic and Roberto Sandoval would turn out to be one and the same person.

Nor would he have suspected that easygoing and down-to-earth Rob would have turned into what looked like a movie star—sleek, polished and overawing.

As they met in the doorway, he was ill prepared for Rob's handshake turning into one of those up-close-and-personal bro hugs.

Just the sensation of having Rob's body collide with his made his entire being tighten and tingle, even though their clasped hands were between them.

"Man, it's good to see you after all these years." Rob's eyes seemed to gleam with sincerity, but Jonah couldn't figure out why.

After all, they hadn't been very close friends back then. Not only had Jonah been a year behind Rob in college, but for the most part Rob had hung out with a far cooler group than Jonah.

And it sure looked like they would still be moving in very different circles now.

Jonah had never felt more provincial than he did standing beside this elegantly put-together man.

"Provincial" had been one of the worst things his grandmother could call anyone, and it made Jonah want to wince to know it applied to him in this situation.

"It's good to see you too," he replied, carefully extricating himself from Rob's iron grip but retaining the sensation of hard muscles and the scents of leather, cologne and something deeply male. It made him have to swallow to clear the sudden constriction in his throat. "Come on back to my office and let me see if I can find you some scrubs. My shirts would fit you, but you're too tall for the pants."

"I can always work in my jeans," Rob replied,

following Jonah down the corridor. "And I'm pretty sure your shirt will hang on me like a curtain. You're pretty ripped."

Silly to feel a glow of pride, hearing the other man describe him that way, and Jonah hid it with a deprecating, "I'm trying to stave off the middle age spread I hear so much about."

Rob's chuckle washed over him like warm honey, reminding Jonah just how much he'd liked that rich sound in the past.

"I've been lucky so far," Rob replied. "But I have to watch it too. Obesity runs in my mother's family, and who knows what the gene lottery has in store for me going forward."

As he opened the door to his office, Jonah gave Rob a skeptical glance.

"I doubt you'll have a problem with that. You look pretty much the same as I remember you from college."

Rob said, "Knock wood," and rapped his knuckles on the door as he went through, making Eunice lift up her head and give a tentative *woof.*

"It's okay, girl." The elderly golden retriever's tail beat a tattoo on her bed at the sound of Jonah's voice, but she also kept her milky gaze fixed on Rob, uncertain about the stranger.

"Oh, hi there, sweetheart." Rob's voice dropped

low and silky, and Eunice reacted to it pretty much the way Jonah wanted to, by wagging her tail even harder and grinning as only a golden could. Rob moved forward to crouch and offer the dog his hand to sniff. "What's your name?"

"This is Eunice." After giving the dog a quick scratch behind her ear, Jonah went to the cupboard behind his desk to rummage for some scrubs. "She's thirteen now, so she spends most of her day snoozing in here while I work."

"Wow. She's doing well for her age. You've taken really good care of her."

Eunice actually deigned to get up, so as to cuddle close to Rob and try to lick his face. He was playfully fending her off, but Eunice was suddenly determined, in a puppyish way Jonah hadn't seen her display for months.

"Well, my mom made sure of that, until she passed a year ago." A pang of sadness made his chest clench, but he was so used to it now, Jonah rode right through it. "Eunice was so depressed after Mom died, I wasn't sure she'd make it, but here she is."

Not wanting to see the sympathy he was sure would be in Rob's eyes, he'd addressed the last of his words to Eunice who, hearing his tone, turned her wiggly, happy attention to him. He bent to accept her licks and snuffles.

"I'm sorry to hear about your mom."

They were crouched on either side of Eunice, who was going back and forth between them, and Jonah reluctantly met Rob's gaze. There was sympathy there, for sure, but also understanding that, somehow, made it bearable.

Jonah found himself giving the other man a half smile—something he'd never have thought himself capable of when talking about his mother at this stage.

"Thanks. She was ill for a long time though. Multiple sclerosis. And she was dreading the end stages, you know? So, when she died, I was sad, but just for myself. Not for her. She didn't want to live like that."

Rob's eyes were like liquid bronze, soft and kind, and Jonah wanted to look away but couldn't.

"Family is everything, right? And the worst part of any loved one having a degenerative disease is watching the progression and knowing there's nothing you can do to stop it. The sense of impotence, when all you want to do is take it all away."

That cut way too close to the bone. Overwhelmed, Jonah rose and held out the scrub top toward Rob. If he allowed himself to think about it, to even agree to the oh-so-true statement, he thought he might cry. Which was ridiculous. He hadn't cried since his mother's funeral.

"Here you go. And let me go see if I can find you some longer pants from the storage closet."

Rob rose too, smiling again, but with a rueful tilt to his lips.

"Don't bother. Even if my jeans get filthy, it wouldn't be the first time I've had to double-wash my clothes. Nothing like being called out to a large animal birth when you're not really prepared for it."

That made Jonah snort in agreement, but he was already at the door.

"I'll just be a minute. No use getting your fancy clothes dirty."

As he rummaged for an appropriate pair of scrub pants, he ruefully admitted to himself how snarky he'd sounded, but he'd been unable to help it. Having to accept Rob's help—even when he knew he really needed it—just made him feel even more of a failure on an already hard day.

Besides, where did the other man get off, looking so damned prosperous and gorgeous?

Stupid. Coming into a small town like Butler's Run dressed like he was walking the red carpet.

Stewing on those sour thoughts helped take his mind off how attractive he found Rob.

Still. After ten years.

That had been a nonstarter back then, and no doubt would be one again.

When he got back to the office, Rob had taken off his jacket and hung it up on a hook by the door. After taking the scrub pants from Jonah, he cocked an eyebrow.

"Should I change in here?"

Jonah froze, forgot how to breathe, realized he'd probably have a heart attack if Rob undressed in front of him and quickly said, "There's a bathroom just down the hall. Left outside, then the first right."

The sound Rob made sounded suspiciously like a snicker, but since he was heading for the door Jonah couldn't see his face to be sure. Heat flared in his chest and up into his cheeks, and he rounded his desk to flop into his chair, relieved to have a few minutes to himself to get his bearings.

Then he realized he had a chance to do a little clandestine research, and pulled his phone out of his pocket. Quickly plugging in *Vet Vic*, he was surprised by the plethora of videos that came up—some free, some on streaming services. Clearly Rob had been busy at it for quite a while.

And all the places he'd traveled to while doing it! All over the States, and even into Canada and

Mexico. There was no mistaking the harsh spurt of jealously that burned bitter in Jonah's heart as he glanced down the list of programs.

Now that was a life. Not this truncated, stagnant existence he was living.

*The only way to grow and to understand the world is to travel through it,* his grandmother always said. *It makes you complete in ways nothing else can.*

Jonah felt stuck, unfulfilled and, yes, incomplete.

But not for too much longer, he promised himself again.

Not that he regretted having postponed his dreams. To do that would also be to regret the time spent taking care of his mom, and that had been a true privilege. As Rob had said, in the final analysis, family was everything. Besides, although it was never quite enough for his own satisfaction, he'd done some good work here in Butler's Run.

He was still scrolling through the list of videos when Rob came back into the office and tossed his clothes over the back of a chair. Jonah couldn't help noticing how the scrub top stretched tight across his shoulders, and his thighs filled out the pants with little room left over.

The slender young man he remembered had

definitely filled out some, and in the best possible way.

Dragging his thoughts away from checking Rob out physically was a lot harder than he wanted it to be, so when he spoke, his words came out harsher than necessary.

"So, what's with the whole Vet Vic thing?"

Rob paused in the act of putting his hair back at his nape with a band and sent Jonah a startled look, no doubt because of the tone of the question.

"I'll give you the short version now, and the long when we have more time. My sister Beeta was in film school and about to graduate in 2019. Since she was planning a career in animal photography and videography, she asked me to help her make a short film. I agreed, and it grew from there."

The envy Jonah felt intensified, but he suppressed it, not wanting to bark at the other man again. After a deep breath, he admitted, "That sounds amazing."

Rob shrugged and gave a grimace. "It's not as exciting as it might look. Long days, sometimes out in the middle of nowhere. Constant travel from one place to the next. It all takes a toll, after a while."

Sounded like heaven to a man who'd hardly

left his small town for more than a couple of days a year, and hadn't had a chance to go anywhere much, but Jonah bit his tongue. No need to let Rob know just how pathetic and insular his life had been since they last saw each other.

Rising, he bookmarked the Vet Vic page on his phone and said, "Let's get going, before the clients start rioting out there."

"I'm yours to command," Rob replied, sketching the kind of exaggerated bow seen only in cheesy movies.

Jonah chuckled, but deep inside, that irrepressible, lusty part of his psyche that he usually kept buckled down tight took notice—and wished he meant that literally.

There were a bunch of things Jonah would love to command Rob Sandoval to do, none of which had anything to do with veterinary medicine!

Rob was a great believer in fate and synchronicity, and could only think that Beeta getting the opportunity to come to Butler's Run fell straight into those categories.

He'd told his sister he was finished with the whole video and documentary thing, but she'd gotten a request to do a piece on the Carolina

Marsh Tacky equine breed and asked him to reconsider.

"The contract specifies you participate, since you're the face of the series so far," she'd said. "I doubt they'd agree to have someone else take your place."

"Did you tell them beforehand that I wouldn't be available?" he'd asked, and he knew from the way Beeta refused to meet his eyes that she hadn't.

"Not really," she admitted, finally looking straight at him. "After all, we've been in this together from the beginning. How was I to know you'd suddenly decide you don't want to do it anymore?"

She'd known, since he'd been saying it for a while, but Rob didn't bother to argue the point with her. Beeta knew he had a hard time saying no to her, and they both knew she was taking full advantage of that fact in this instance.

Their collaboration had been financially lucrative for both of them, but Rob was tired— bone tired—of the constant moving around. The rootlessness and loneliness of traveling, of never being in one place for any length of time. Even when he'd had a chance to go home to LA, his apartment felt barren and sad.

Plus, there was her insistence that he always

look like he'd stepped out of a fashion magazine when in public. That part of it he particularly hated. Especially like here, in a rural setting, when he'd fit in far better if he'd been wearing the clothes he did when he went back to visit his parents on the ranch.

He'd stuck out like a sore thumb, and Jonah's little digs about his appearance hadn't gone unnoticed. He was trying to avoid reacting, but it had been hard.

After all, if he hadn't seen Jonah's name mentioned in the briefing the Marsh Tacky folks had sent, he'd definitely have refused to come. It was as though he were being sent a sign.

He'd been so discontented with his life, and seeing Jonah's name had taken him back to a simpler time. One where he was charting his own course, rather than following someone else's, where he could just be himself, and not this mythical person, Vet Vic.

"Just this last one," he'd told Beeta firmly. "Then I'm done, for real. You've made the name for yourself you needed to get your career on a solid footing, and it's time for me to go back to my life."

"I have," she'd replied, but from her tone and earnest expression he'd known he was still in for an argument. "Producers and investors know I'm the brains behind the innovative camera work, but you're the one everybody recognizes in the streets. We have such a good thing going, I can't believe you want to give it up. What are you going to do? Go back to clinical work?"

That's exactly what Rob wanted to do, although Beeta had looked skeptical when he said so.

They may be brother and sister, and share a love of animals and the outdoors, but beyond that, they were completely different.

Beeta had always been independent, with itchy feet and the kind of driving personality that sometimes had her butting heads with others—from their parents to strangers on the street. Rob, however, liked a quieter, more laid-back life, which made him more cautious. Beeta would jump into things with both feet and fight her way through whatever came next, but Rob found that kind of lifestyle too stressful.

*Think first, act later* was his mantra.

Rob looked around as he followed Jonah down the corridor, toward the back of the clinic. There were three exam rooms coming off the hallway, and another door marked as storage. Ahead of them he could see a general exam and treatment area, with tables, an X-ray room and two glass enclosed operating rooms.

People were bustling around, smiling at and greeting Jonah, and giving Rob the once-over. Everything was neat, and clean, and looked like heaven to him.

This was what he'd been craving over the last eighteen months, and lucky Jonah Beaumont had it all. A place to call his own, surrounded by people he knew, serving the needs of animal owners he was familiar with.

The longing that swamped him was almost crushing. His life had been anything but stable over the last four years, and he craved the security of having a home again, wherever it might end up being.

"Hey, y'all," Jonah called out. "Come on over here a second." As they gathered around, Rob noticed two of the techs nudging each other and sending sideways glances his way. When everyone had closed in on where they were standing and fallen silent, Jonah said, "This is Dr. Rob Sandoval—a friend of mine from vet school. He's agreed to help us out today, since we're short-staffed. He'll be working alongside me, kinda as a vet tech, since he's not listed on our insurance, so don't be asking him to operate on any animals, okay?"

There was a smattering of laughter, and a round of introductions, starting with the associate vet, Dr. Inez Nguyen, all the way down to a timid-looking teenager, who mumbled his greeting toward the ground.

But it was that same youth, Alan, who asked, "You're Vet Vic, aren't you?"

"Yeah, I am." No call to pretend otherwise. "But only when I'm being filmed. Otherwise, you can call me Rob."

"Okay, Dr. Rob."

Alan still hadn't looked up at him, but Rob smiled at the youngster anyway, and didn't object to the more formal name.

"Oh," Jonah added. "Somewhere around here is Gilligan, our office cat. Where is he, Alan?"

"In the hospital, Dr. J.," Alan replied. "Making his rounds."

"His rounds?" Rob looked from one face to the other, wondering if they were messing with him.

"Yeah." It was Alan who answered, giving him a brief glance, before his gaze dropped once again. "He likes to visit the animals. Seems to make them feel a bit better."

"Sounds like a solid member of the team," Rob said, delighted at the mental image of the cat going from cage to cage, offering comfort to other sick animals.

"He is."

"All right, y'all. Let's get back to work," Jonah called. "Sam, you work with Dr. Nguyen on Geoffry—I think he's in for a parasite check—and Dr. Rob and I will deal with whoever's next on the list."

The packed waiting room should have alerted Rob to the pace of the clinic, but he was still surprised by the number of patients they saw that morning. And the variety of animals.

"You have a lot of exotic animals coming through here," he remarked to Jonah while they sat in his office during a brief break, munching on muffins someone had brought in. "I've never treated an Egyptian uromastyx, even in the clinic in LA."

Jonah gave a little shrug, which included a sexy little tilt of his head that Rob couldn't help noticing, although he knew it wasn't smart to be thinking about the other man that way. So far Jonah's reaction to him was less than welcoming, and Rob was smart enough to take a hint.

Wasn't he?

"I've seen a lot more exotic animals being kept as pets since the pandemic," Jonah replied. "I don't know if people had more time to search for interesting animals or what, but I've had more unusual reptiles, rodents and mammals in the last four years than I'd seen any time before."

"Bet some of those textbooks from college came in handy," Rob teased, wanting to see Jonah smile.

He was rewarded when the other man laughed outright.

"Some of them had to be replaced. They fell apart. And then, one night I fell asleep before taking Eunice out for her walk, and she peed on the last of them." He shook his head. "I couldn't be mad at her. It was my fault."

They were on their way back to see their next patient when the receptionist came barreling down the hallway, a frantic look on her face.

"I just got a call about a dog that—I'm not sure—I think they said it got stung by wasps?"

"Calm down," Jonah said, putting his hands on her shoulders. Poor girl looked as though she was about to burst into tears. "Take a deep breath. What did the owner say, and where are they?"

After following his instructions and inhaling a massive lungful of air, the young woman said, "I couldn't understand all of it. Someone was shouting in the background. But I know I heard something about wasps and the dog's tongue being swollen. They're on their way in to the clinic."

"I'll go out and meet them," Rob said and, without waiting for a response, strode down the corridor toward the front of the clinic.

"Hey, Vet Vic," called one of the men in the waiting area. "Are we going to get to see the doctor anytime soon?"

"I'm sure Dr. Nguyen will be with you in a moment," he said, not breaking stride as he headed to the front door. "We have an emergency coming in any second."

There were a few murmurs, but no one complained. At least not that Rob heard before he went out the door. They'd probably expect the same diligence if the injured animal coming in were theirs.

Going out the front door, he paused to scan the parking lot and driveway leading to the clinic, but there was no one there. So, leaning a shoulder against the wall, he took a deep breath of the warm spring air. Set back from the road, and surrounded by what he figured was at least an acre and a half of land, the clinic gave the impression of being in the middle of nowhere, even though it was right off the main thoroughfare. At the corners of the front of the building were two peach trees in glorious bloom. The pink blossoms exuded their delicate honey-almond scent, which, with the odor of freshly cut grass, merged into an almost intoxicating mix.

Rob took another deep breath and felt more alive and happier than he had for a long time.

Then he shook his head and smiled.

*Jonah Beaumont.*

He'd had a massive crush on Jonah back in vet school, but there'd been a distancing bubble around the other man, and Rob was unwilling to do anything to try and breach it. For a while he wasn't even sure Jonah was gay, since he'd kept himself firmly to himself. Ironically, it was only at the end of one semester, when he'd seen Jonah at a club dancing with another man, that he'd been sure.

But thereafter, although he'd flirted shamelessly with Jonah, there'd been little reaction. Then, before he could work up the courage to openly approach him, Jonah was gone.

Now, working alongside the other man, Rob had realized just how good a vet Jonah was. Not just in the way he handled and treated the animals, but in the way he connected with the owners too.

He wasn't overly jovial, but he was the epitome of politeness, patience and gentleness. When he smiled or laughed, he lit up the entire room. And more than once Rob had found himself fixating on Jonah's wide-palmed hands, whether while he was examining an animal or gesticulating while he spoke.

Rob found himself rubbing his left arm, where goose bumps had suddenly appeared, despite the sultry air.

He couldn't help wondering what those hands would feel like running over his body, finding all the most sensitive places, making him lose himself in sheer pleasure.

With a grunt and a shake of his head, Rob pulled himself back from those thoughts.

Yes, he was attracted to Jonah, but no, he wouldn't pursue him.

He was already wondering if coming here had been a mistake, a misguided rush of nostalgia that had kept him on the same track he'd been so determined to get off of. Whether it had actually been born of his fear that he'd never get his life back to where he wanted it to be. Or fear of the unknown, after so many years of being towed along by the freight train of Beeta's ambition.

Was there actually a place for him, somewhere?

And if so, where?

The craving for stability was visceral, and almost always top of his mind. Jonah had what

Rob wanted, which begged the question: was that what Rob was really attracted to, rather than the man himself?

He needed to figure that out, rather than just concentrate on the desire he felt in Jonah's presence.

Just then a pickup came careening off the road into the driveway, and he waved it up to the front door, moving to meet it as it screeched to a halt.

No more time for daydreaming, no matter how sweet the fantasy may be.

# CHAPTER THREE

THE DOG, A ROTTWEILER or Rottie mix, jumped out of the back of the truck, but staggered when it hit the ground. Rob could see the dog couldn't close his mouth, and when he got a front view of its face, he realized the tongue was so swollen it looked like a huge pink sponge.

The woman was sobbing as she got out of the passenger side, and the male driver looked like he was on the verge of a breakdown, literally spinning one way then the other, rather than bringing the dog in.

"Will he try to bite if I pick him up?" Rob asked, taking the leash from the owner's hand.

"I was trying to get rid of—"

"Hang on," Rob interjected, realizing they were too frantic to be of much use just then. "Let's get him inside, and then you can tell Dr. Beaumont what happened."

Taking a chance, hoping the dog wouldn't

struggle much, he bent and picked him up, grunting at the sheer weight of the animal.

"Get the door," he ordered, as he moved as quickly as possible to the building. "And don't forget to turn off your truck."

The woman ran ahead and held the clinic door open for Rob. Thankfully, the dog put up no resistance to being carried, and as he hurried through the waiting area, he heard the murmurs of the other clients.

"Have you brought your dog here before?" he asked the woman, who was opening the door leading to the exam rooms.

"Yes," she answered, tearfully.

"What's his name, and yours?"

"He's Bear, and I'm Maggie Cole. My husband is Chad."

"Laura," he called as he hurried past. "Please pull Bear Cole's file. His owners are Maggie and Chad Cole. Bring it back ASAP."

Jonah was hurrying down the hall toward them, and Rob heard the door from the waiting area bang open behind him too. No doubt Chad Cole rushing to catch up.

"What happened to Bear?" Jonah asked, turning to keep up with Rob and listening for the answer over his shoulder. He bent slightly, so as to visually examine the dog's mouth, as Chad replied.

"There was a wasp's nest on the shed soffit, and I decided to get rid of it. When I knocked it off, Bear grabbed it and ran off. By the time I found him, he was chewing on it."

"Did you use pesticide to get rid of the wasps?"

Rob couldn't stop himself from asking the question, even before Jonah could, and he sent the other man an apologetic glance as he put the dog on the table. Jonah didn't seem to notice or care though as he stuck his stethoscope into his ears.

"No. I never use pesticides on the farm. We're organic growers. I burned them out."

That, at least, was a relief. Bad enough to be dealing with the venom from the grubs still in the nest. If there was also a pesticide involved, it would make the situation that much more perilous.

Rob was already at the drug cupboard when Jonah said, "Epinephrine. And bring the oxygen. His breathing is labored."

Rob grabbed the medication Jonah asked for, as well as antihistamine, and took both back to the table.

Poor Bear was lying there, his eyes wide and pitiful, and after Rob handed Jonah the epinephrine and antihistamine, he stood by the dog's head and encircled its neck with one arm.

"You're going to be okay, Bear," he crooned, wanting to keep the dog calm while Jonah injected the epinephrine into the muscle on his flank.

"This is to help him breathe easier, and get his blood pressure where it needs to be," Jonah explained to Maggie and Chad, as he gave Bear the shot. "And I'm going to administer an antihistamine and a steroid injection. Those'll work over time to help him recover."

One of the vet techs brought the oxygen apparatus, and Rob took the mask and placed it in front of Bear's nose, while the tech got the flow going. The animal's breathing was still labored, no doubt obstructed by the massive tongue. If it didn't start to shrink soon, they would have to intubate or, worst-case scenario, do a tracheotomy.

"There isn't much more we can do right now. I want to keep him here for a while, to monitor him. We'll call once we have an update," Jonah said to Maggie and Chad.

"Oh, but can't we stay with him?"

Maggie's eyes were filled with tears, but Jonah shook his head. Softly, he replied, "I'm afraid we just don't have the space for you to be back here for any length of time. We'd have to be working around you, and that wouldn't be safe for any of us. Don't worry," he added, putting an arm around her shoulders and his hand on Chad's arm. "We'll take good care of him and let y'all know as soon as there are any changes." Turning to Rob, he asked, "Do you mind keeping an eye on Bear for a while?"

"Not at all." Jonah probably wanted the clients out of the room, in case they had to intubate or insert the tracheostomy tube. With the couple already so upset, that would be extra traumatic for them.

"But you'll check on him too, won't you?" Chad asked Jonah, his lack of confidence in Rob's abilities as clear as if he'd voiced them.

"I will," he replied, then added, "But this is Dr. Rob Sandoval. He's a vet too, so Bear is having the best possible care he can right now, even if I'm with another patient."

"Oh." Maggie's eyes widened in surprise. "I hadn't heard that you brought in another vet."

"It's a long story," Jonah replied, easing both the Coles toward the door. "But I'm sure you'll hear all about it very soon."

And, as they walked away, Rob couldn't help silently chuckling to himself.

Yep. Small-town life summed up right there.

\* \* \*

Jonah tried to go on with his day as though nothing untoward was happening, and thought he was doing a pretty good job—despite the way his pulse leaped each time he exited an exam room and glimpsed Rob keeping vigil at Bear's side.

There was something intensely appealing about the way the other man stroked the dog's fur and whispered into his ear. Plus, Gilligan, the black cat, was perched on Rob's lap, his face on the edge of the examination table, close to Bear's. He might be there to offer his version of care, but Rob was also stroking his back at the same time, so Gilligan was getting something in return too.

It took a while for Bear's breathing to even out and for there to be a visible reduction in the size of his tongue, but Jonah was able to call Maggie and let her know the dog seemed to be out of the woods.

"We're gonna keep your baby here for a while longer," he said when she asked if she could come and pick Bear up. "But unless there's a deterioration in his condition this afternoon, you can come and get him before six, when the clinic closes."

Like a trout caught on the end fishing line,

Jonah found himself drawn back to Rob's side, although there was no need for him to be there.

"Hey," Rob said, giving Jonah one of his cheeky smiles. "He's doing a lot better. O-sat is good, and he can almost close his mouth, although he hasn't gotten control of his tongue back yet. Respiration is smooth, heart rate within normal parameters too."

"I told Maggie she could come get him before the clinic closes, unless there's a change for the worse. Looks like he's out of the woods now though."

Rob stroked the dog's head and got a gooey, love-struck glance from the Rottie mix.

Jonah shivered, thinking he'd probably do the same if Rob Sandoval touched him that way.

Dragging his mind away from the abyss it seemed determined to stand on the edge of, Jonah turned back toward the exam rooms, then paused. Facing Rob once more, he said, "I think he'd be okay in a kennel now, with periodic checks. You must be hungry. Why don't you go get something to eat?"

It was already after two thirty, and the clinic was finally slowing down, but with Bear's emergency neither of them had had time to get food since having muffins earlier.

"I'm okay," Rob said, getting up off the stool

he'd been sitting on and stretching. Jonah looked away quickly on seeing the scrub top rising, revealing a strip of what appeared to be a most delectable belly. "What about you? You haven't eaten either."

Jonah shrugged, ridiculously touched that the other man was concerned for his welfare, even in such a small way. The people around him were kind and considerate, and more like family, but they seemed to believe he was more than capable of looking after himself.

"I'm used to working through lunch. Even if you're not starving, there are some snacks in my desk if you want to take a breather and have some."

"Keep an eye on this guy for me a moment," Rob said, gesturing to Bear, "while I get a kennel ready for him. And why don't we have an early dinner together, when the clinic closes? I just heard from my sister, and there's some issues she has to deal with before we can start filming, so I'm free both tonight and probably tomorrow. If you need help again, I'm available."

Oh, he needed help all right, but not at the clinic…

Someone needed to give him a quick rap over the head so he'd stop lusting after Rob and keep his mind on business.

He should refuse. Make some excuse not to go or to have Rob back the next day. Spending the day with Rob had been both pleasure and torture. The other man's easygoing character, sly humor and obvious care for the animals threatened the tight control Jonah kept on his needs and desires.

Rob Sandoval, in short, confused the heck out of his world, and Jonah didn't like it.

Or he liked it too much.

Hard to know which, when his brain seemed determined to drop down into his shorts whenever the other man was around!

Hopefully, after a short while, Rob and his sister would be gone, and Jonah could get back to normal.

Boring ol' normal sounded both good and horrible right now. Considering how badly he wanted some adventure in his life, you'd think he'd be glad of this sudden turn of events, but this wasn't the kind of excitement he'd expected.

Yet, even as the thoughts barreled through his mind, he heard himself say, "Sure. Sounds good. And I'll be glad of the help tomorrow too."

"Awesome." Rob's smile set Jonah's heart thumping again. "How about Lonie's Café? I noticed it on the way through town earlier."

Jonah only just stopped himself from grimacing. Lonie, proprietor of the café, was his aunt, favorite relative and the one person in the world who could read him like a book. Sometimes like a kid's picture book, at that.

"We could go there," he said, trying to find a way out of what felt like a situation he wasn't ready to face. "Or we could drive fifteen minutes up the road and go somewhere nicer."

Rob lifted Bear off the table like the dog weighed nothing at all, and Jonah saw the way the muscles in his back flexed with the action. Mesmerized, he hardly heard the other man's words.

"Is the food at Lonie's not good?"

Now Rob was bending to slide Bear into the low kennel, and Jonah tried to force his gaze away. But there was no escaping the allure of Rob's lean, toned body in motion.

"My life wouldn't be worth a hill of beans if I said it wasn't," he answered, his mouth on autopilot as he tried to get himself under control. "It's my aunt's restaurant."

Rising, Rob looked over at him, that impish smile playing around his lips, his eyes gleaming with amusement.

"So, you don't want me meeting your aunt? Is that why you're reluctant to go there?"

"It's not… I just…" What was it about this

man that reduced him to a blithering idiot? Worse, he'd hit the damn nail on the head too, which was completely unfair. Jonah allowed annoyance to overcome attraction and, in an act of sheer self-preservation, came up with what seemed to him a completely reasonable excuse. "I eat there all the time. Kinda thought it might be nice to get out of town instead."

Rob's amusement didn't abate, and one eyebrow jumped, as if querying the veracity of Jonah's words.

"Next time," he said, his voice dropping a little, as if not wanting to be overheard. Which was silly, since they happened to be the only ones in the room. "Tonight, I'd like to see more of the town. And meet your Aunt Lonie."

There was an undercurrent in his words, impossible to ignore or pretend not to hear. It gave them a kind of heated intimacy that made Jonah want to run, or to hide.

Or to grab Rob and kiss him until they both exploded into flames.

Scared, aroused, confused, Jonah turned on his heel and headed for his office, saying, "Whatever. Just let me know when you're ready to go."

It sounded rude. He knew it did, but he couldn't make himself feel ashamed.

As he dropped into his desk chair, leaned his head back and closed his eyes, Jonah wondered why it felt as though his world, which had previously been staid, boring and way too settled, was all cattywampus.

*Rob Sandoval.*

Something about that man turned Jonah inside out.

Always had.

He'd had the hots for Rob back in vet school, but Jonah had been determined to keep his eyes on the future he dreamed about. Traveling and treating animals around the world. Learning about different cultures, while saving endangered species. He couldn't afford to be distracted by anything, or anyone—not even a man with the most alluring eyes he'd ever seen, and a mouth made for loving.

So he'd made it a point to not take Rob's flirtations seriously, or even really acknowledge them.

"You can only control your life if you control your emotions and urges," his grandmother had told him when he was a young teen. "That ability is what truly separates humans from animals."

Back then she'd been lecturing him because of a fight he'd gotten into, but he'd somehow known she'd meant it as a life lesson, and he'd taken it to heart.

And it was just as well he had, since it had only been a few more months before he'd had to leave Southern California and move back home. That would have been much harder if he'd been romantically involved with Rob and leaving him behind.

Now the damn man was back in his life, and already making waves, rocking his world in ways both big and small.

Looking way more delectable than he had a right to.

Charming everyone, from staff to clients—including Jonah himself.

And, worse, showing his absolute competence around the clinic.

A little part of Jonah had been hoping Rob had fallen back on the whole Vet Vic thing because he couldn't make it in the competitive world of veterinary medicine, but clearly that wasn't true. He'd not only shown his capabilities, but even preempted Jonah a couple of times with questions and treatments that were completely on point.

Considering how determined Jonah was to always be in charge, he should resent the way Rob had of quietly taking over, but somehow couldn't.

It was a real conundrum.

Sighing, shaking his head to try and clear it, Jonah tried to think about his plans for the future. Goals that had sustained him for years, and brought him joy, even when his reality was in shambles.

But instead of seeing himself traveling, free to go wherever he wanted, all he could see was Rob smiling. And the yearning that vision created was even stronger than any of his oldest dreams could engender.

# CHAPTER FOUR

HAVING HEARD THE dismissal in Jonah's voice, Rob stayed out of his way for the rest of the afternoon, instead offering his services to Inez Nguyen, which were accepted.

"Today was shaping up to be rough until you stepped in," she said, as they took a cat suspected of swallowing a hair tie back to X-ray. "Thank goodness we didn't have any surgeries scheduled, or we'd have had to either cancel them, or one of us vets would have had to work the crowd on our own."

"Is it always this busy?" he asked as he put on the lead apron.

"Not always. But Dr. Beaumont is really popular, and everyone knows if you want the best care, this is where to get it." She gave him a clear-eyed glance. "That's why I'm here, instead of in Charleston with my family. Working with Jonah will be a boost to my reputation."

While he positioned the unhappy feline on the

X-ray detector, holding it still, Rob considered what Inez had said.

It was a little strange to think of this relatively small clinic, in a very small town, having the kind of reputation she'd intimated. Not that Rob didn't believe it possible, although he wondered how it had come about.

Jonah had been at the top of his class when they were in college together, so it wasn't surprising to realize he'd become a great vet. How his reputation had grown beyond the borders of his obvious purview was another thing entirely.

"How did you find out about this place?" he asked, trying to sound as though he were making small talk, although curiosity was burning away inside.

"Jonah is known as an equine and exotic animal expert in the state," she replied, squinting at the X-ray, now projected onto the screen in front of her. "Even though he'd deny it, he made a name for himself during the year he spent at the Cricket City Zoo, just outside of Charleston. He's also the official vet for the Carolina Marsh Tacky Association, doing all their genetic testing and everything else. Since taking over this clinic, he's poured himself into it, and people noticed."

Another facet to an already complex character, Rob mused. Coming from a farming community himself, he knew the local vets had to be well-versed in a wide variety of animals, but the breadth of knowledge Jonah obviously had was amazing.

"But you're an all-rounder yourself, aren't you?" Inez asked, giving him another of those piercing glances. "You'd have to be, to host your show."

"Not really," he replied honestly, although he knew Beeta wouldn't like to hear him say so. She was all about his so-called image, constantly saying he had to maintain that air of knowing far more than he actually did, even when off camera. "Remember, I get to do a bunch of research before we film, so I have an unfair advantage. It's not like when someone brings an animal into the clinic presenting with symptoms you've never seen before, and you have to hurry to make a diagnosis."

She nodded thoughtfully, then pointed at the screen.

"What do you think?" Abruptly ending their conversation.

And, thankfully, there was no sign of anything foreign in the cat's digestive tract, so they didn't have to operate.

By six o'clock, when the Coles came to pick

up Bear, the Rottie mix was back to normal, although Jonah made sure to tell them to keep an eye on the dog for any residual symptoms.

"You have my cell number," Jonah told them, while Bear danced around, licking everyone within tongue reach, as if delighted to have use of that organ again. "Call if you're at all worried. And next time, keep him inside if you're dealing with wasps. Clearly, he has a taste for the grubs."

"You bet I will," Maggie said, stooping to hug her recalcitrant pet around the neck, and getting a lively face wash in return. "'Cause you know this goofball won't have learned his lesson."

They were the last clients to leave, and the staff wasn't far behind, calling out goodbyes as they went.

Then there was just Jonah, Eunice and Rob left.

"I have to take Eunice home and give her a little walk," Jonah said, still sounding distant. "Want to meet me at Aunt Lonie's?"

"Sure," Rob said, although he'd been about to suggest they ride together. "How long do you need?"

"I'll be there in thirty minutes, God willing and the creek don't rise. By that, I mean as long as Eunice cooperates."

Rob couldn't help chuckling, even though Jonah was already walking toward his truck. And he stood and watched the other man gently lift the aged golden into the back of the vehicle before he turned toward his rental.

Once inside, and after Jonah had driven off with a toot of his horn, Rob sat for a while without starting the vehicle.

It had only been a day, and not an overly eventful one at that, yet it felt as though he'd experienced a seismic shift, and he couldn't figure out why.

Maybe it was just being in a place where he felt at home? At peace?

Where—although he'd grown up a continent away—he had no problem understanding the mindset of the people he'd met?

He refused to consider that it had anything to do with Jonah Beaumont.

Realistically, although Jonah looked almost the same as he had ten years ago, and despite the attraction Rob still felt toward him, they were actually strangers.

His earlier thoughts and questions had stayed with him throughout the rest of the afternoon, and he'd decided it was his overwhelming yearning to once more belong somewhere that was messing with his head.

What a relief it had been to be able to do his job without fanfare or any kind of false adulation. Years of pretending to be someone he wasn't had taken its toll. All he wanted now was peace, quiet and a place to belong.

But he wasn't quite there yet, and he couldn't afford to allow his libido—or any other emotions—to add additional problems to the mix.

Once he found a place to settle down, all this angst would retreat.

It didn't take him long to drive to Lonie's Café, or to find a spot to park on the main thoroughfare. There were a few cars scattered on the street and in a parking lot farther along the way, but clearly Butler's Run wasn't a happening place on a Wednesday evening.

Lonie's was a long, rectangular room, with well-worn dark wooden floors, round tables and a counter with a brass rail and tall stools along one side. Behind the counter was a pass-through to the kitchen, from which emanated such delicious smells Rob's stomach rumbled, loudly. Thankfully that was covered by the strains of new country coming through hidden speakers.

Three tables were occupied, closer to the back of the room, but Rob chose one overlooking Main Street, wanting to enjoy any people-watching opportunities that may arise. By the time he sat down, the waitress came bustling over.

"Hi, there, honey. Welcome to Lonie's. My name is Carmen, and I'll be your server. Can I get you something to drink?"

"Just water for now, please, Carmen." Rob smiled up at the young woman, taking the menu she held out. "But can I order an appetizer while I wait for my friend to join me? I'm starving, and the food smells are killing me already."

Carmen chuckled, nodding, as if this was nothing unusual. And it probably wasn't. Rob doubted people walking by could resist coming into the restaurant, even if they weren't hungry.

"Give the menu a quick look then," she said. "And I'll get Ms. Lonie started on whatever you want."

"What do you recommend?" Rob asked in return, scanning the beginning of the menu but not being able to make a choice.

"We got in a fresh catch of crayfish today, and Ms. Lonie makes the best crayfish balls you've ever tasted."

"Oh, yeah." Rob's stomach rumbled again, making them both laugh. "I'll definitely have some of those."

"You got it."

As Carmen headed back toward the kitchen, Rob turned his attention to the street outside, his mind going straight back to Jonah Beaumont.

There was a reticence about Jonah that intrigued Rob in a way he couldn't resist. Hidden depths of character he sensed couldn't be readily understood, but would need to be teased out, little by little. Yet, why he wanted so badly to be the person to draw those secrets out, Rob couldn't say.

Sighing, he rubbed the bridge of his nose. He always tried to be honest with himself, which Beeta said was one of his worse habits, since it led to far too much of what she called "navel gazing." His sister was more the action type, eschewing introspection for constant movement. Rob needed to understand himself, at the very least, to be truly comfortable with his own needs and feelings. Understanding other people was a lot harder, but he knew if he could get even an inkling of someone else's motivation, connecting with them became easier.

But he still wasn't sure why, exactly, he wanted a connection with Jonah to begin with. It could be just that Jonah's life in Butler's Run so closely mirrored what he wanted for himself that Rob was drawn to get to know the other man better. Doing so would help him figure out how to build the future Rob wanted, the one Jonah already had.

Yet that didn't ring true either.

Rob already had a pretty good idea of how to get to where he wanted to be. All that was left to be decided, as far as he could tell, was where, exactly, to put down new roots. While there were questions he could ask Jonah about the running of a clinic like his, that wasn't what he was curious about.

No. What he wanted to know was far more personal.

Intimate.

Like whether he was involved with anyone, and why he kept such a distance between himself and the people around him.

Or was it just Rob that Jonah kept at arm's length? Now that he thought about it, Jonah had an easy way with his clients and staff, with none of the snark he'd thrown Rob's way.

It was a bit off-putting to think there was something about him that made Jonah act that way.

Both Carmen—with his crayfish balls—and Jonah arrived at about the same time, interrupting Rob's reflections.

"Hey, beautiful," Jonah said to Carmen, bending to kiss her cheek. "I see you've already met Rob."

"Not officially," Carmen said with a grin. "But I knew who he was. Emma Gorman was in earlier. Told us all about seeing Vet Vic and convincing you to let him help at the clinic."

Jonah's lips twisted, and he exchanged a knowing look with Carmen.

"No doubt."

"Lady with the pink hair?" Rob asked.

"Well, ain't you the smart one?" Carmen said, giggling, while Jonah chuckled too. "How'd you know?"

Shaking his head, Rob replied, "I come from farm country, so I know how small towns work. I never met her, but she was the most vocal one in the waiting room this morning. Seemed like a pretty good guess."

"Will you two stop jaw-jacking and let that man eat his crayfish balls, before they get cold?"

At those words, all three of them at the table turned to watch the diminutive lady marching from the kitchen toward them, with what looked like a ferocious scowl on her face.

She was dressed in a black chef's coat, wearing a small cap and matching pants in a Kente-inspired pattern, and there was no mistaking her air of command. The resemblance between

Jonah and his aunt was marked, with both having the same complexions, noses and shape of mouths. But where Jonah's eyes had that sleepy droop, his aunt's were large and wide, and lighter brown than her nephew's impenetrable darkness.

"Uh-oh, Mom's coming," Carmen muttered to Jonah, grinning. "You're in trouble now."

"Nah," he replied, pinching Carmen on her side, as his aunt got to the table and Rob rose to his feet, earning himself a swift glance from the older lady. "Aunt Lonie loves me. I'm her favorite nephew. Isn't that right, Auntie?"

"You're my only nephew," the older woman replied tartly, even as she held her face up for Jonah to kiss her cheek. "And a sassy-pants to boot."

"Sassy-pants." Carmen sing-songed the words through her giggles, earning another pinch from Jonah and a narrow-eyed look from her mother.

"What you standing around for, girlie? Think the customers gonna go back into the kitchen for their own food?"

With one last giggle, Carmen headed off toward the other occupied tables in the restaurant, and Rob found himself the focus of Jonah's aunt's full attention.

"So you're the famous Vet Vic, huh?" Her tone

was curious rather than rude, and it made Rob smile.

"Just plain old Rob Sandoval, ma'am," he replied, holding out his hand, which was quickly clasped in her tiny but firm grip. "It's a pleasure to meet you."

"Ooh, and so polite too," she said, giving him a grin and looking about as young as her daughter with it. "We might have to keep you around, just to teach these other young'uns some manners."

"Hey," Jonah said, putting his hands on his hips. "That's not fair. I'm a perfect Southern gentleman."

"Huh." Lonie's grunt spoke volumes, and made Rob have to hold back a laugh. "Rooster today, feather duster tomorrow."

That was too much for Rob, and he couldn't stop his amusement from showing. Bending, he kissed her hand, then said, "Ms. Lonie, you are a gem beyond price. I'll do my best to smarten this fellow up while I'm here, just for you."

"You do that," she said, as she gave his fingers a quick squeeze at the same time that she whisked the menu off the table with her other hand. "Now, sit you down, both of you, and I'll send you out some food. Chef's choice."

"Thank you, ma'am," Rob called as Ms. Lonie

marched off toward the kitchen, getting a flap of her hand in reply.

As they sat down across the table from each other, Jonah sighed. "Well, you've got Aunt Lonie's seal of approval."

Rob smiled, not sure why that made him feel so good. "Why'd you say that? We hardly got a chance to chat or get to know each other."

Jonah shook his head, his lips twisting—this time in obvious amusement rather than anything else. "If Aunt Lonie doesn't know you, or can't get a read on you, she waits to see what you order and makes a decision based on that. When she offers to choose for you, it's because she likes you." He grinned. "And it also means she's about to send out enough food to feed the Gamecocks football team, so I hope you're real hungry."

"I definitely am." Unable to resist anymore, Rob cut into one of the crayfish balls. When he put the first piece into his mouth, his eyes all but rolled back in pleasure. When he'd chewed, savored and swallowed, he said, "OMG, I'm so up for anything your aunt wants to feed me."

Glancing up, he found Jonah staring at him in a way that made heat fire down his spine, and had goose bumps rising all over his chest and arms. Those usually sleepy eyes were even more hooded, but his expression was anything but slumberous. Instead, there was an intensity to the concentrated way he kept his gaze trained on Rob's face, and his lips were tense, causing two lines to form on either side of his mouth.

Frozen, Rob could only stare back, their gazes clashing for what felt like forever, but couldn't have been more than a couple of seconds. Then Jonah looked away, breaking the spell holding Rob captive.

Completely frazzled, and now unsure of what exactly just happened, Rob stuffed the other half of the crayfish ball into his mouth to give himself time to calm down.

For a moment—a crazy, lust-inducing moment—he'd thought he'd read longing in Jonah's expression. But, when he looked across the table again, there was no sign of anything like that on Jonah's face anymore.

Maybe he'd imagined it?

But the tingles still tiptoeing up and down his spine seemed to whisper he hadn't.

"Good, huh?"

Jonah's voice was normal, with a hint of amusement, causing Rob to intentionally match his tone.

"Amazing. Here." He pushed the plate to the middle of the table. "Have some."

Jonah reached for one and popped it whole into his mouth.

Rob quickly looked away, not wanting to have his gaze snared by the sight of the other man's mouth.

*Libido running amok again. Calm down.*

Although the thought was meant to settle him down, it didn't really help. And he was relieved when his phone rang, giving him a necessary distraction.

"My sister Beeta," he said to Rob. "Forgive me, but I need to take this."

"No problem." Jonah started to get up. "I'll give you some privacy."

"No need," he replied, hitting the button to start the call and gesturing for Jonah to stay where he was. "Hey, Beeta."

But, as he listened to his sister bring him up to date on what was happening with the proposed documentary, Rob almost wished he'd let Jonah get up, or that he'd gotten up and taken the call outside.

He could have used a brief respite from the tension he was experiencing from just being in the other man's presence.

# CHAPTER FIVE

JONAH KEPT TRYING to train his gaze elsewhere, but it returned to Rob over and over again.

The sight of Rob eating that first bite had thrown Jonah completely for a loop.

If he'd thought his world felt cattywampus earlier, that was nothing in comparison to what it felt like now. As though he were sitting not on a chair, but in a puddle of shifting, waving sand, threatening to pull him down into a place he both feared and desperately wanted to be.

Looking down at the table where his fingers drummed, seeking to alleviate some of his angst, he couldn't help wondering if, when their eyes met, Rob had felt the same lightning strike of desire. The surge of arousal had damn near incinerated every sensible atom in Jonah's body, making him long to reach across the table and kiss the taste of the food off Rob's lips.

Learn Rob's own special taste.

He'd lusted at first sight before. After all,

that was kind of a prerequisite when you'd re-
signed yourself to one-night stands and occasional booty calls far from home. Traveling to
Atlanta, far enough away he'd be pretty sure not
to see anyone he knew, meant limited time to
spend on making any but the most superficial
connections. He hadn't been looking for anything solid or lasting anyway.

At this point in his life, he wasn't even sure
if he'd ever want a relationship. Not only would
it be another rope to tie him down, but the part
of him that had always known there was something lacking within himself constantly whispered he'd be courting disaster to even try.

It wasn't something he'd be able to explain,
had someone asked, but even as a child he'd
known he somehow wasn't enough. That despite
his best efforts, he could never fulfill other people's needs or expectations.

Imagine giving himself over to another, just
to be told he was somehow deficient. Not suf-
ficient to make and keep a man he loved happy.

It had even happened once, long ago, and although he'd eventually gotten over it, the thought
of going through that again was way too distaste-
ful to be contemplated.

Thankfully, just then Rob finished his call,

so Jonah was forced to pull himself out of those torturous thoughts before they went any further.

"Everything all right?" he asked, seeing the thoughtful look on the other man's face.

"The documentary is on hold, at least for another few days. One of the participants lost a mare and wants some time to recover, and the town council is hemming and hawing over the permit we need to film the Easter Marsh Tacky parade. Beeta was assured it would be issued without any problem, but now it's in question."

There. If Jonah needed a reminder of his own shortcomings, he'd been smacked in the face by the mention of Marnie Rutherford's mare. All amorous thoughts and feelings drained away, to be replaced with a wash of cold reality.

No skirting around it though. It wasn't in his nature to hide from difficult truths.

"Marnie had mentioned to me that she'd be participating in the documentary, and she'd planned to have Night Wing feature prominently in the film. Losing her was a tragedy."

"I'm sure it was."

The sincerity in Rob's tone, along with his not asking any probing questions about the mare's death, was somehow exactly the response Jonah needed. A little of the stress released from his shoulders and chest, and he took a sip of water before continuing with the conversation.

"As for the permit, I'd guess the bugbear is Henry Aitkins. He's on the council and also a Tacky aficionado, and he's been complaining about the documentary to anyone who'll listen."

Rob's eyebrows rose questioningly. "Do you know why?"

"He's worried that increasing the Tackys' profile might attract the wrong kinds of breeders. The type that just want to make money off the horses by saying how rare they are, etcetera."

"Ahh."

Rob was leaning forward, his arms crossed on the table, and he nodded. Suddenly, Jonah realized he was mirroring the other man, and that by doing so their faces were very, *very* close together. He could see the tiny lines at the outer edges of Rob's eyes, the way the light played off his cheekbones and the humorous, sexy tilt of his lips in fine detail.

God, he was beautiful.

"I hope y'all are hungry." He'd been so enthralled he hadn't heard the kitchen door open or his aunt approach. Swiftly leaning back in his chair, avoiding Aunt Lonie's gaze, Jonah pretended a great interest in his cutlery.

"Ms. Lonie, whatever that is, it smells divine."

Rob's crooning tone drew Jonah's gaze like a gecko to a moth, and once more he was forced to quickly look away from the other man, not wanting anyone—especially Lonie—to notice he was staring.

"And it'll taste that way too," Lonie replied, as she shifted dishes from her tray to the table.

"Mom's not known for her modesty," said Carmen, as she also unloaded a tray of food, until the tabletop was almost covered.

"Course not. I'm known for my cooking," was the swift and tart reply. "We've got some braised short ribs, chicken fried steak, potato and leek mash, collards, fried okra, fresh biscuits and gravy. And make sure you save space for dessert. I have a mixed berry pie that'll knock you into next week."

Rob's warm laughter spiked right through Jonah, leaving him dry-mouthed and wondering if, famished as he was, he'd be able to eat. His stomach was in knots.

"Thank you, Ms. Lonie. I wouldn't mind a quick time travel experience."

That drew amused chuckles from both his aunt and cousin, and Jonah forced himself to join in.

What he really wanted to do was run out the door, before Rob cast more of a spell on him.

That, or grab Rob and take him somewhere private, so he could find out if he was the only one feeling this dangerous, delicious pull.

Neither of which was possible just then. Nor advisable.

So, he settled his napkin more firmly on his lap and braved a look up at his aunt.

"Thanks, Auntie."

She nodded, putting a hand on his shoulder and giving him a sly, knowing grin.

"Don't thank me yet. Wait until that man falls in love with the food. It'll make him want to stay around forever."

*Crap.*

His aunt was always on him to get involved in a relationship. It had been that way since he was in high school and still dating girls. It was only after his grandmother died that he confessed, first to his mom and then to Lonie, he was gay. Neither had cared, but Lonie had her own slant on it.

"Just means you have to find a nice *man* to settle down with, instead," was her sanguine reply. As if she'd always known, but hadn't wanted to broach the subject until he did.

Now he was sure she'd seen through his casual facade to the interest he had in Rob.

That didn't bode well for the next couple of

weeks. She'd be all over him like a leisure suit, trying to find out whether there was anything going on, and she'd be disappointed when he told her no.

"I think you're right, ma'am." Rob was piling his plate with food, his smile wide and unfettered. "Can I just move in here? Be your greeter and busboy? I'm a really bad waiter though—found that out in college—so I won't volunteer for that job."

"I'm sure someone can situate you more comfortably," Aunt Lonie replied, squeezing Jonah's shoulder again. "But you come by and see me whenever you want. I'll keep your stomach happy."

Then she and Carmen were gone, leaving Rob and Jonah alone together again.

"Aren't you going to eat?" Rob paused, knife and fork in hand, to give Jonah a concerned look. "You didn't really have anything much today. Aren't you starving?"

"Yeah." Jonah tried for a smile as he started dishing out his own dinner. "I was just lost in thought for a moment."

They ate silently for a while—or silently if you didn't count Rob's sighs and quiet moans of pleasure with each mouthful. Jonah tried not to hear them, but they were completely, utterly distracting.

He wanted to be the one causing those sounds to issue from Rob's throat—drawing them out with touches and kisses and…

*Wow! No!*

Dragging his brain away from those fantasies, he searched desperately for something innocuous to say.

"You don't seem very upset by your sister's call." Thank goodness for the subliminal brain, which apparently hadn't been fogged over completely by lust. When Rob cocked an eyebrow at him, Jonah elaborated. "Hearing that the documentary is being delayed."

Rob swallowed, took a sip of water, then replied, "I'm not. Honestly, I didn't even want to do this documentary at all."

"Really?" After all the different videos Rob and his sister had made, what was it that made him not want to do this one? Probably the ridiculous small-town location, Jonah thought. And who could blame him? Butler's Run was the epitome of insignificant, except in the eyes of its inhabitants.

Maybe he shouldn't feel that way about his hometown, but he couldn't help it. There was an entire world out there to explore and experience. Why would anyone want to come here?

"Yeah." Rob met Jonah's gaze, and his expression was suddenly completely serious. "I'd told Beeta I was through with the videos from last year. That I wanted to stop traveling and find a spot to settle down."

"She didn't believe you?"

Rob huffed. Not quite a laugh but a mixture of amusement and annoyance. "She knew I meant it, but she also knew I have a hard time saying no to her, so when this opportunity came up, she took it without consulting me."

Hard to believe that Rob would want to give up a lifestyle Jonah would give his eyeteeth to have, or that the other man would be a pushover for his sister.

Unable to restrain his curiosity, he asked, "Why would you want to give up making the videos? It looks like you've done well with them."

"We have," Rob admitted readily. "I'd have never believed I could make that much money from something like that. But it's not for me, long-term. I need a certain amount of stability in my life, you know? And being on the road for so long that I even had to send my dogs to live with my brother because I was never home doesn't provide that. I want to get back to clinical work and have a place to call my own."

Jonah considered that for a few minutes, thoughtfully chewing a mouthful of steak while he did.

"I guess you've been doing it for a while." Rob had said the videos started in 2019. "But it's still difficult for someone on the outside to understand why you'd give it up. So many people are dying to be internet famous. Or just plain famous."

Rob's lips tightened slightly, and he shook his head.

"Sure, but I was never one of them. I've made good money from it, but it's cost me as well."

"Your dogs?"

"Sure. And a relationship, back in 2020. And a life beyond airports, rental cars and motel rooms, if I'm lucky to be sleeping in one, and not out in the middle of nowhere in a tent. When I finally go home to my apartment, you know what I find? Emptiness. Nothing. Not even a potted plant to give the place a little life. I've moved around so much, there's been no opportunity for meeting anyone and having any kind of meaningful relationship."

The near ferocity in his tone told the story even more broadly than his words. While Jonah was coveting Rob's life, the very experiences he longed for were soul destroying to Rob. Jonah felt a wash of sadness and compassion for the other man.

"I…" He hesitated, wondering whether Rob would appreciate being commiserated with. But he went for it anyway. "I'm sorry it's not working out for you. And that it caused a breakup." Although he couldn't understand why anyone would break up with Rob.

Rob shrugged, but Jonah wasn't fooled. There was still a brooding cast to the other man's face, which told him it still hurt.

"It was during the pandemic." He sighed, slowly spearing a piece of okra but not putting it into his mouth. "The clinic I was working at closed, and Beeta suggested we hit the road and do more videos. Andy—my ex—was an accountant and started working from home, and I think it irked him that I was out and about while he was trapped in the apartment. One day I came home and he was packed and ready to go." His lips quirked. "At least he waited for me to get back and didn't just desert the dogs."

"That sucks." Although Jonah was kind of glad Rob didn't have a significant other in his life just now.

Not that he was planning to make a move on the guy, but it was good to know anyway.

"I'm over it," Rob said, a determined note, and a finality, to the words. He smiled, eyebrows rising. "What about you? Any special someone waiting for you at home?"

"Other than Eunice? No. Frankly, there are only four gay men other than me, that I know of, in this town, and I'm not interested in any of them. Not that I'm looking for a relationship anyway."

"Oh?" Closing his knife and fork, Rob pushed his empty plate aside and gave Jonah an intent stare. "What's wrong with the men here?"

Glad he hadn't homed in on the fact he wasn't looking for a relationship instead, Jonah readily answered, "Gerry's at least eighty, John and Marlon are married, and Tony…" How to explain Tony? Six feet three inches tall, mountain man beard, with a bit of a mean streak. "Tony's just not my type."

Rob had his elbows on the table again, leaning in, giving the conversation a level of intimacy Jonah couldn't help but notice. The hair on his nape prickled, and it took every ounce of control he had not to lean forward too. Get closer to those now copper-colored eyes and quirking, sexy mouth.

"What is your type?"

Rob's voice was low, a murmur. Sinful and inviting.

Was Rob interested in him, sexually?

Jonah's head reeled at the thought, and then he caught himself.

Rob had always been like this—seemingly flirtatious, sexy as sin and twice as tempting— but Jonah reminded himself not to fall into the trap of thinking it was personal. It hadn't been ten years ago when they'd first met, and it definitely wasn't now either.

Swallowing, battling between prevarication and deflection, he decided, instead, to be honest.

"My type is someone far from Butler's Run, who isn't interested in anything more than a night or two of uncomplicated sex."

Rob's eyes widened.

"Damn. Okay."

"Did I surprise you?"

"I don't know why, but you did."

He'd surprised himself too, if he were being honest, but Jonah wasn't going to admit that to Rob. Normally, he was completely mum on anything to do with his sex life, not wanting to give the town gossips anything to talk about. Maybe it was because Rob wasn't from here and was simply transient that made it easy to talk to him about it.

"In a place this small, it makes sense to keep my…activities…elsewhere," he said, warmth rushing up from his chest at the way Rob was staring at him. "It's not like I can sneeze here and everyone not know."

That made Rob chuckle and nod. "I remember, from when I was a kid. I hated it then—that feeling of always being watched—but I miss it now." He waved a hand, his mouth rueful. "Not the always being watched part, but knowing most everyone around and being a part of a community. In LA I wouldn't recognize most of my neighbors if they walked up and bit me on the nose."

"Sometimes, I think I'd like to be anonymous like that," Jonah admitted. "I felt like that at UC Davis, and it was freeing, to be honest. When I had to leave, it sort of felt like coming back to a cage."

Rob's expression was intent. "Why did you leave anyway? You were acing the coursework, and then, poof, you were gone between one year and the next."

"My mom got sick, and the doctors didn't know how the disease would progress. Although Aunt Lonie was here with her, I wanted to be as close as possible, since we didn't know how long she had, or how much help she'd need. I transferred to a college nearby. Thankfully, although I lost my scholarship, my grandmother had set up a trust for all her grandkids' education, so my tuition was covered."

Rob smiled, a soft tip of the lips. "You're a good son. There are a lot of people who'd make every excuse—including there being other family nearby—to go on with their lives, regardless."

Why that filled him with pride was a question for another time.

"I'm an only child, and it was just the two of us since I was little. I just did what I had to. Not that it made much of a difference."

With a tilt of his head, Rob questioned, "How can you be sure? She lived quite a while after that. Maybe she wouldn't have, without your support."

How to respond to something that goes straight through your heart, lightening it to the point where you feel as if it would float away?

Jonah looked down so Rob wouldn't see how moist his eyes had become, and he was struggling to find a reply when he was saved the effort by Rob's phone dinging. From beneath his lashes, he watched as the other man picked it up and read something on the screen.

"Oops. Beeta's back in town and wants to discuss how to move forward on the project," he said, laying the phone back down before getting to his feet. "I'm going to have to run. Let me go pay for the meal."

As he got up, Jonah replied, "You can try, but I think Aunt Lonie will have something to say about that."

Rob chuckled as he walked away, and Jonah let out a long breath as soon as the other man was out of earshot.

That off-kilter feeling had intensified as the evening went on, and he was equal parts glad and unhappy to have their time together end. He really needed to get his head on straight when it came to Rob Sandoval. Otherwise, the week or however long the other man would be in Butler's Run would be excruciating.

"He's handsome." Carmen had come over so quietly Jonah hadn't even been aware of her approach. "And charming too."

With a silent sigh, Jonah agreed with his cousin. "He's all that."

"Gay?"

"Yeah, but please don't tell your mom. You know how she gets on my case."

Carmen snorted. "If you think she doesn't already have it sussed out, you don't really know your auntie."

"Ugh." Jonah looked up at Carmen and caught her sympathetic look. "There isn't anything between us. And there can't be."

She shrugged as she piled their empty dishes onto her tray.

"Don't see why not, but you know your business best."

Jonah couldn't help smiling at her. They'd grown up together, and Carmen was the closest thing he had to a sister. Closer than one, maybe, since there wasn't much they didn't talk about together.

"Thanks for that. And if you could just convince Aunt Lonie…"

That earned him another snort. "Fat lot of good that would do, *mon ami*. You know she has a mind of her own, and a stick of dynamite won't change it."

Unfortunately, he was well aware of that fact.

Rob came back just then, two carryout containers in his hand.

"Not only would your aunt not take my money, but she also gave me two pieces of pie for us to take home." He shook his head, grinning, as he handed Jonah one of the cardboard boxes. "How was I to say no to her?"

"You can't," both Carmen and Jonah said at the same time, which reduced them all to laughter.

After saying good-night, Rob left, and Jonah followed right behind, forestalling the grilling he knew his aunt was itching to give him. Getting home, he took Eunice out for a quick ramble, then settled down in his home office with his pie, telling himself he'd look at the pile of bills he needed to get paid within the week.

However, when he turned on his computer, it wasn't to open the accounting software but to go to the channel where some of the Vet Vic videos were available.

Rob Sandoval was stuck in his head, and maybe seeing him over and over on film would begin to inure him to the man's presence.

*Yeah. Sure.*

And he was so enthralled he didn't even register how delicious the pie was until he was finished and the taste lingered, tantalizing on his tongue. Not unlike the way Rob lingered in his mind.

# CHAPTER SIX

THE NEXT MORNING Rob got to the clinic at seven o'clock—earlier than Jonah had suggested, but since he'd been awake since six, he figured he might as well. Besides, unless the clinic was very different from the ones he'd worked at before, there'd be at least one person there, checking on the overnight dogs, beginning the cleaning process and preparing for the day.

So it was no surprise there were three vehicles in the parking lot at the side of the building, one of which was Jonah's truck. Seeing it ignited a spark of excitement deep in Rob's belly that was impossible to ignore.

He'd spent most of the previous night thinking about Jonah—about his complicated personality, his life story and the intense attraction Rob felt toward the other man. There'd been moments when he was sure Jonah felt the same pull toward him, but then a curtain would come down behind those sleepy, sexy eyes and shatter Rob's certainty.

Jonah was a master of concealing his emotions, making Rob want, more than ever, to break through the barriers surrounding the other man.

Sometime in the night he'd realized that all thoughts of keeping his distance were slowly fading into the background. And no matter how many times he tried to remind himself not to get too involved, he couldn't ignore his own interest in Jonah.

He'd been touched by the other man's devotion to his mother, and surprised to hear him confess to seeking sexual encounters away from home. In his head, after spending some time together, Rob had been sure Jonah would have been snatched up by some lucky guy long ago. After all, there was absolutely nothing wrong with the other man, as far as Rob could tell.

He was kind, successful, smart and sexy as hell.

And sure, Butler's Run was a small town, with not much opportunity to meet someone and develop a relationship with them, but this wasn't the nineteenth century. There were so many other ways to meet other people—online dating sites, mixers, even matchmakers—and he couldn't figure out why Jonah hadn't gone any of those routes.

If there ever was a man who deserved a stable and happy home life, it was Jonah. Just seeing him interacting with his aunt and cousin showed the love between the three, and how much he cared about them. He even gave up being a student at a prestigious school to be there for his ill mother. Those natural attributes would translate wonderfully into a more intimate relationship, Rob was sure.

Or was he projecting his own desires onto Jonah?

Maybe he didn't want that kind of closeness, or a life partner. Not everyone did, although Rob couldn't really understand why. Wasn't life better with someone to share it with? Someone to depend on, and who depended on you?

Although it had been so long since he'd been intimate with anyone, Rob wouldn't turn down a night or two of no-strings sex. It wasn't usually his thing, but if Jonah were to offer…

Rob drew himself up and muttered a curse.

That was no way to start the workday. Especially when the subject of his lust was one of the people he'd be working with, closely.

*Not as closely as you obviously want*, the irrepressible part of his brain whispered, propelling him out of the vehicle.

Hopefully having something to do with his hands would quell this obsession with Jonah.

When he got to the side door, he found it open and stepped inside. Alan was there, as was Jada, one of the other techs.

"Mornin', Dr. Rob." Jada smiled at him as she thrust an armful of towels and drapes into the washer. "You're here early."

"Just thought I could help get things set up," he replied, wiping his feet before starting across the floor. "Do you know what's on the agenda today?"

"Eight surgeries this morning," Alan replied, looking from the list in his hand to the rolling tray beside him, which held a variety of cleaning equipment already in place. "I'm finishing up the dog kennels."

"Is Dr. B in his office?"

"Yep," Jada said. "Go on through."

Rob forced himself to move at a normal pace through the back part of the clinic, past the overnight hospital cages, X-ray room and surgical suites. Yet, a sense of anticipation made his strides just a little longer, and his heart was racing at the thought of seeing Jonah again.

Outside the office door, he paused to take

a deep breath and compose himself. Then he knocked.

"Come."

"Good morning," Rob said, as he walked into the office, receiving a grunt in return from Jonah, who was staring at his computer screen, and little *yip* of welcome from Eunice.

At least one of them was glad to see him, Rob thought, annoyed at himself for being let down by Jonah's lack of enthusiasm. Rather than sit down, he went to stoop beside Eunice and began to make much of the sweet senior.

"How did your meeting with your sister go?"

Apparently Jonah was ready to acknowledge his existence.

"Okay. She was considering whether to stay and battle it out with the council or just call the whole thing off." He wasn't going to admit that he'd argued for giving the project a chance, while Beeta—never the most patient of people— was leaning toward going back to LA. "She finally decided to give it a couple more days, after I gave her a few suggestions on how to frame the project to the town."

Eunice lay back down, so, with a final scratch behind her ear, Rob rose to step over and sit in the chair across the desk from Jonah. Their gazes clashed, but Rob was once more reminded of Jonah's ability to disguise what he was thinking or feeling. While his heart was racing, and he was sure his desire was written all over his face, Jonah's expression could have been carved from stone.

He looked away, feigning interest in a bit of fluff from Eunice, which he picked off his scrub pants.

"I told her to remind them that the Marsh Tacky is still considered critically endangered, and that a closed stud book exists for the breed. Anyone interested in getting involved in breeding them has to go through one of a handful of reputable breeders, and the paperwork has to be in order. Our documentary will definitely emphasize those points, and make it clear that the bloodline of any animal being sold can be checked through the association."

Jonah shook his head, a movement Rob noticed from the corner of his eye, and he forced himself to look at the other man.

"I don't see why that would deter anyone who wants to start breeding them."

"The object isn't so much to deter additional people getting involved with breeding the horses, but to show it's not an easy occupation to get into. It's not like buying any old horse, or horses. It's a carefully overseen process, with a DNA bank and oversight from different associations. Scammers want something easy. And anyone seeing the documentary will go away from it fully informed."

"Hmm..." Jonah leaned back in his chair, his hands clasped at his nape, his gaze drifting across the ceiling. "Okay. That sounds like a valid argument."

"I also suggested that she request you join the shoot."

Jonah's feet hit the floor with a thump.

"Me?" His eyebrows were up almost at his hairline. "Why?"

"Well, my understanding is that you're the foremost expert on the Marsh Tacky, from a veterinary point of view. If you're involved, I think the dissent will fade away."

Jonah didn't say anything for a few long moments, his gaze searching Rob's face. In his expression there was what Rob interpreted as a hint of excitement.

Was what he'd said the day before about fame—how so many people craved it—something he felt, himself?

"What did your sister say to that?" he finally asked, eyelids drooping to hide his gaze, the curtain back in place.

"She thought it was a good idea and told me to ask if you'd be interested."

"Let me think about it," Jonah said, as his computer pinged, and he leaned forward to look at the screen. "In the meantime, knowing I had a slew of surgeries scheduled today, I emailed my insurance company last night and asked about putting you on my policy, temporarily. This is the rep getting back to me to say she checked your credentials, and she's made the insertion, so you're on your own today, as a vet here."

It was exciting and frustrating at the same time. He'd been looking forward to working closely with Jonah again, but it was a good chance to get back into the swing of things.

Besides, Jonah obviously didn't share his eagerness, a fact that irked Rob a lot more than it should.

But he made sure to keep his voice even when he said, "Great. Inez and I will hold down the fort while you're operating. What do you have on the table?"

Jonah clicked through to a different screen on his computer and said, "Three spays—one of which is a rabbit—two neuters, a canine aural hematoma, a lipoma—that I'm hoping is non-infiltrating—and cystotomy stone removal on a cat that came in yesterday." He frowned slightly, his lips twisting downward. "Those are always tricky, so I explained to the owners that the outcome was no better than fifty-fifty and let them take their baby home to love on her last night, just in case."

"How old is the cat?"

"That's the problem," Jonah replied, pulling on his chin. "It's eight, so not so young anymore. Anesthesia will be tricky, and recovery isn't a given."

"Well, good luck." Rob glanced at his watch and stood up to stretch. "I'm going to go through and make sure I'm completely familiar with where everything is. Don't want to look like a bumbling fool in front of the clients."

"The techs know where everything is, even if you don't."

"Where I used to work, we didn't have techs come in with us all the time when we examined patients, so I'm used to muddling through on my own. It wasn't as fancy as your setup here. But then, we were dealing with pets, not a patient like Geoffry the goat."

He smiled at the other man, hoping for a smile in return, but was disappointed. Jonah was still frowning at his computer screen.

"Yeah. Farm animals definitely need an additional pair of hands."

Feeling dismissed, and put out, Rob grunted in reply and bent to give Eunice one last pat.

After all, he thought as he left the room without another word, it wasn't the golden's fault her owner was being a jerk.

Jonah sat back in his chair and exhaled the breath he felt he'd been holding since Rob walked into the office.

Seeing the other man had had his pulse racing and his body reacting like a teenager.

In fact, he couldn't remember a time when he'd reacted this way—libido out of control, driving him nuts—since his teen years. Since the summer he turned eighteen and had his first romantic encounter.

*Remember how that turned out...*

The thought should have quashed the arousal racing like lava through his system, but, although it cooled it somewhat, such was Rob's effect on him, it couldn't douse it completely.

With a groan, he rubbed at his face with both hands, trying to force himself back to normality. He had a full schedule ahead. Delicate surgeries that demanded his complete attention. Allowing Rob's presence to shake his cool wasn't an option.

After the other man was gone—*please, Lord,*

*soon*—he'd definitely need a trip to his favorite club in Atlanta. Although he wondered if he'd find anyone able to arouse this kind of desperate interest. Even though he wasn't into relationships, in the past there'd always had to be a higher level of personal interest. Not emotional, but definitely physical.

But no one had ever exerted such a strong pull on him before.

Who could match up to Rob Sandoval?

Eunice groaned, got up and tottered over to lay her head in his lap, looking up at him with her wise, liquid gaze. Grateful for the comfort, he scratched behind her ears the way she liked.

"I wish you could talk, Eunice. I get the feeling you'd have some really great advice to give me. Maybe even be able to tell me what Mom would say, if she were still here."

Eunice's tail swished slowly, and her mouth opened in a grin.

"What do you think I should do—about Rob, and also about his sister's request that I take part in the documentary?"

It was easier to think about the latter, which didn't have the power to upend his life the way the former did.

Having watched the videos the night before, he knew he didn't have the charisma that had made Vet Vic so popular. Rob's easy warmth and charm translated perfectly to the screen, while Jonah knew himself to be far more detached and reticent in character. Yet, it was certainly tempting to get a taste of Rob's world, even though he'd be a mere bit player.

And it was even more tempting to think that, if his participation would sway the council, it would keep Rob around for a bit longer.

Although, if he were in his right mind, he'd want the other man gone ASAP.

Eunice grumbled, gave his hand a lick and wandered back to her bed.

"Yeah," he said, rotating his shoulders and neck to loosen up the muscles. "I guess it is time for me to get to work."

As he made his way to the surgical suite, he forced his brain away from his personal life and onto work. No matter what else was going on around him—or in him—the animals always came first, and he was determined to do the best he could for them.

And he didn't have much time to ruminate as he and his surgical staff went through the cases, starting with Mona the cat's bladder surgery, which thankfully went well. In between two of the spays, he went to check on her and saw Rob rushing two medium-sized puppies into the isolation area.

"What's up?" he asked.

Without stopping, Rob turned a grim face his way to reply, "Parvo. Bad cases."

Following him, Jonah paused at the door to the isolation unit. "Crap. How old?"

"The owner isn't sure. He was told they were eight weeks old, but it's hard to tell. They're pretty undernourished and could be younger. Do you have the CPMA treatment?"

"We do," he replied. "We signed up to be a test site, because of the prevalence of parvovirus in this area."

The new intravenous medication, using monoclonal antibodies, had been approved for the treatment of parvovirus, but it was only for dogs eight weeks old and over. If these pups were too young, they would have to be treated the way they'd always treated infected animals—with fluids to counteract dehydration, medication to combat the symptoms and a whole lot of luck.

"Should I administer it?" Rob asked.

"What do you think?" Jonah asked, wanting to hear Rob's opinion.

"With the virus load, and their otherwise poor condition, I think I'd take the chance on giving them the treatment, since it's available. I doubt they'll survive otherwise."

"Go for it," he replied, somehow trusting the other man's judgment. "Jada knows where it is."

But there was no time to stop and ask anything more, as Cliff, who was administering the anesthetic for the surgeries, called out to say the next patient was down and ready.

It was late in the afternoon before Jonah finished up the last surgery, because they'd also had an emergency come in, and he'd had to put the dog with a severely lacerated paw into the rotation. When he'd paused for lunch, there'd been no sign of Rob, and he'd avoided asking about him. The staff might not have thought anything of it if he had, but he had formulated the idea in the back of his head that he needed to wean himself off the other man.

That way, when he left, it wouldn't be so much of a wrench.

But, as the end of the day was drawing close and Jonah was checking on his surgical patients, he casually asked Cliff, "Hey, have you seen Dr. Rob?"

"He just finished up with his last patient, and I saw him heading to isolation."

Checking on the parvo pups, no doubt.

Jonah hesitated, vacillating, and then, with a

sigh of resignation, went that way. It was, after all, his clinic. His name on the board outside. The patients were his, no matter who else was looking after them.

When he opened the door, he saw Rob sitting on the floor, leaning toward the cage where one of the puppies lay, gently stroking the small inert form with his gloved forefinger. Just his posture alone showed his concern.

"Any improvement?"

Rob looked up and gave a little shrug.

"I think so, but that might just be wishful thinking. They're on fluids, anti-nausea and pain meds, and I gave them a dose of antibiotics and a wormer. But they were in such poor condition when they got here, I think they came out of one of those damned puppy mills, from what the owner said."

Jonah moved into the room, letting the door close behind him. Then he lowered himself to sit beside Rob. The puppies were fluffy and looked to be some type of toy breed, although it was hard to say which one. Both were on drips to try to keep them hydrated, since the vomiting and diarrhea associated with parvovirus would cause dehydration and potential organ failure. The monoclonal antibody treatment was supposed to help prevent that though.

"What did the owner say?"

"That he saw an ad on the internet, saying the breeder had shih tzu pups for sale. When he expressed interest, the seller told him to meet them at a gas station, rather than having him come to their home. The pups looked bright and lively, and he fell in love with them and bought both."

"Yeah, that does sound sketchy." Jonah reached into his pocket and took out a pair of gloves. After putting them on, he opened the second cage and reached in to pick up the other pup. It was heartbreakingly thin beneath its fluffy coat, and hardly reacted at all to being lifted. After closely examining it, he added, "I don't think this one is a shih tzu at all. Looks like a mix."

"I agree," Rob said with a frown. "I told the owner that, and he was so disappointed. But he also told me that he hopes they pull through, because he's gotten attached. Apparently, his wife passed away not long ago, and he got the dogs for company and, as he put it, a reason to get out of bed in the morning. He named them Milo and Ovaltine."

Jonah grunted, not knowing what to say to that. Eventually, he came up with, "Well, you're doing the best you can for them." Placing the puppy back in the cage, Jonah added, "It's time to close this place up. Most of the staff is probably already gone."

Rob nodded but didn't move. "If it's okay with you, I'm gonna stay here a while. Keep an eye on these two. Lock up, and I'll call you when I'm ready to leave, if that'll work?"

"Sure. If that's what you want."

"Yes. I won't stay long."

But as he got up to go to the door, Jonah looked back at Rob and had a feeling the other man planned to stay the entire night, nursing the puppies.

It was just the kind of dedication and caring he'd expect from him.

And damn him for being so appealing in this nonsexual, lovely way.

# CHAPTER SEVEN

ROB STOOD UP and stretched, trying to get the feeling back in his leg. A glance at his watch showed it was just past six. Beeta had been texting him, asking where he was. She planned to go to dinner with her assistant and assistant cameraman over in Hilton Head and wondered if he wanted to come. Of course, he'd refused the invitation, although his belly reminded him he hadn't eaten since lunch. He wanted to be here in case he needed to adjust the puppies' meds, and just in case the worst should happen despite them being given what had been called a "miracle" treatment for the virus.

Although the circumstances weren't ideal, there was a certain feeling of rightness being here, taking care of the babies. It had been so long since he'd been invested in the well-being of specific animals. It felt like coming home to be able to devote his time and energy to these pups.

They were both sleeping, their respiration was

even and the little hearts were still beating away, albeit a bit too fast for his liking, but he felt confident enough in their condition to take a little break. Although one of the vet techs had brought him a cushion before they left, so he wasn't sitting directly on the concrete floor, he needed to move a bit. And a bathroom break wouldn't be a bad idea either.

Walking to the bathroom, it occurred to him just how comforting it was to be back in his own milieu, rather than in Beeta's world of camera angles and close-up shots. If he'd needed a sign that his intention to leave that all behind was right, he'd certainly got it.

He needed the ebb and flow of real life around him. The sense of community and commitment he felt existed in places like Butler's Run. Even his crazy desire for Jonah made sense in that light, since, if anything could come of his longing it would—in a perfect world—create the ideal life.

Partnership with a man as devoted to animals as he was, in a town that could give him the peace and stability he craved after his crazy life on the road.

The fact that it probably wouldn't happen didn't really matter. He'd enjoy these sensations and the feeling of doing something worthwhile for as long as it lasted. Besides, there was also the excitement of truly *feeling* again. Of longing for connection, both emotional and physical, with Jonah.

It brought him alive in a way he hadn't been for a long, long time. And what was so terrible about that?

As he was coming out of the restroom, he heard the sound of the outside door rattling and, startled, stood stock-still for a moment. Walking as quietly as possible, he slipped back into the examination area at the back of the clinic and peered around the corner, toward the side door.

It was Jonah, backing in through the door, juggling a box, his keys and Eunice's leash.

"Hey," he said, moving forward to give the other man a hand. "What are you doing back here?"

Jonah shrugged, surrendering the box and turning back to close and lock the door he'd just come through.

"I couldn't leave you to starve to death," he said. "So I went by the café and got some food. It was that or pizza."

"Either one would work, but your aunt's cooking can't be beat. I really appreciate it."

Warmed by the other man's concern, Rob rested his hand on Jonah's arm and drew in a breath as his palm made contact with Jonah's skin. Heat bloomed in his chest and seemed to jump through his entire body, just from that simple touch.

He could have sworn Jonah was affected too, as he stood frozen in place, his gaze trained down to the point of connection between them. Then he looked up, and, for an instant, Rob saw the flare of desire in Jonah's eyes, and his heart leaped.

At that moment, more than anything else in the world, he wanted to kiss Jonah silly. Make that spark turn into an inferno that would disintegrate the other man's habitual reticence and every other barrier that there could be between them.

Jonah moved away so suddenly Rob was left with his hand still in the air.

"Let's take the food through to the office," he said over his shoulder, walking in that direction. "How are those babies doing?"

For an instant Rob couldn't find his voice because of the mix of desire and disappointment racketing around in his body. Taking a deep breath, he cleared his throat and started after Jonah, replying, "They're still hanging in there."

"That's what I like to hear."

He was already shifting stuff off his desk by

the time Rob made it into the office. Putting the box down on a clear corner, Rob stood for a moment, undecided.

Should he make his interest known to Jonah, or leave it alone?

Normally, he tended to be cautious in his personal life, waiting to see how things developed before exposing his own feelings, but with Jonah there was a strange kind of urgency goading him to act. Maybe it was because of the time constraints? Knowing he wouldn't be around for very long made it seem imperative to admit his feelings. Yet, even with that excuse, it had only been two days since they'd come back into each other's lives. Way too soon to be reacting this way, right?

Jonah looked at him, raising his eyebrows.

"You gonna sit down or what? Don't let Aunt Lonie's food get cold."

Rob dropped into the chair in front of the desk, pushing aside the thoughts twisting through his head. It was really only then that the scent of the food made its way into his consciousness, and he groaned.

"Wow, that smells fantastic. What is it?"

"Hoppin' John, shrimp and grits, fried okra and chicken bog." He paused as he was pulling out containers from the box and shook his head.

"Aunt Lonie never feeds me like this. She really likes you."

Rob chuckled, half rising from his seat to peer into the containers. "I'm thankful for her liking, believe me. But you have to explain what Hoppin' John and chicken bog are, since I've never heard of them."

"Apparently she's trying to woo you with all the traditional South Carolina favorites," Jonah said, handing Rob a large plate with high sides—almost like a combination plate and bowl—and a fork. "Hoppin' John is this one here." He spooned some of the rice mixture into Rob's plate. "Rice, peas, bacon, deliciousness."

Rob's mouth was already watering from the smell, and he wasted no time in taking a bite. The sound that rose in his throat when the flavors burst to life on his tongue was unintentionally sensual, but completely appropriate.

"Oh, sweet merciful father," he said when he'd swallowed. "That's downright sinful, it's so good."

"Try the rest," Jonah said, his lips twitching into a smile. "It's all amazing. But save space for berry cobbler."

"At this rate, I'm going to have to buy a new wardrobe. I can feel my belly growing, just from looking at this feast."

The food had done the trick to dissipate any lingering discomfort between them, and they chatted casually during the rest of the meal, when their mouths weren't full.

"Inez said you worked at a zoo nearby?" Rob asked Jonah. "What was that like?"

"It was amazing," he replied, and there was no mistaking the enthusiasm in his voice. "That's what I'd wanted to do, from the beginning," he continued, helping himself to more grits. "I'd planned to go off to Africa, or Asia, and work with sanctuaries or zoos. Kill two birds with one stone—get to travel and to work with the animals."

It was clear that he'd given up that dream to take care of his mother, and once more Rob was moved by his dedication to family.

"I'm actually thinking of resurrecting that dream," Jonah said. "Now that Mom's gone, there's nothing holding me here, except for Eunice." At the sound of her name, the dog's tail beat a brief tattoo against the floor, but the golden didn't open her eyes. "Once she's…"

His voice trailed off, and Rob nodded, not needing him to finish.

"But what will you do with this place? Seems to me a lot of people around here rely on you to take care of their animals."

"I'll sell it. Hopefully I can find someone capable to buy it, and the clients will be taken care of."

Rob didn't even think it through—the words just popped out of his mouth. "I'll buy it."

Jonah was glad he'd finished what he was eating, because he was so surprised by Rob's pronouncement that he inhaled a huge gulp of air and would have choked if he'd had food in his mouth.

For a long moment he just stared across at the other man, trying to decide whether he meant what he'd said or not. There was no hint of amusement on Rob's face. In fact, he looked excited, eyes gleaming and lips turned up in an enthusiastic smile.

"You're kidding me," he finally said. "Why on earth would you want to do that?"

"It would be perfect," Rob replied, the words almost tripping over each other with his obvious excitement. "I've been looking for a place to call home, and I think this could be it. Of course, I've only been here two days, but what I've seen and experienced so far makes me feel at home."

As Jonah sat there, still in shock, Rob got up to stride back and forth across the office floor, eyes unfocused, as though envisioning the future and speaking it into being.

"I know it sounds crazy—"

"It does," he agreed.

"And impulsive—"

"For sure."

Rob paused, sending him a look that he didn't know how to interpret. "But from what you said, you're not quite ready to sell, so there's time to figure things out."

Leaning back in his chair, completely flummoxed, Jonah said slowly, "Are you actually serious?"

"Completely," Rob replied, back to striding across the floor. "We could start out with me coming on board as an associate, so you can figure out if I'm the right fit. Then, if you wanted, we could discuss my investing into the clinic." He grinned. "You have a lot more expertise with exotic animals, and you can bring me up to speed on how to treat them. Plus, I'd have the benefit of your reputation to help me keep the clinic going after you leave."

Suddenly he paused, both in his pacing and his monologue, and Jonah found himself the focus of a penetrating stare.

"That is, if you decide to leave at all."

Mouth dry, Jonah swallowed before replying, "I plan to."

"But, if you don't, we'd have to have a provision in the agreement to cover that eventuality." He'd been near the door, but now walked slowly closer. "We'd have to come to some arrangement about whether we could still work together."

Rob had stopped at the side of the desk, and Jonah noticed how bright his eyes were, as though behind the bronze depths a lamp had been lit. They were dazzling, hypnotic, their sparkling intensity creating a bubble that encompassed the two men and had Jonah's heart racing. He couldn't break free, even if he'd wanted to.

"Why wouldn't we be able to?" Why did his voice sound so faint, barely rumbling out of his throat?

"Because I'm attracted to you," Rob replied, equally quietly, tightening that intimate bubble even more. Drawing Jonah in, as if a cord stretched between them had shortened, creating a searing drag on his body. "If anything happens between us—of an intimate nature—that would muddy the waters. Considerably."

"I..."

Shock and a rush of intense arousal rendered Jonah mute, and he couldn't even think of what to say. He was lost in those brilliant eyes, the moments stretching on to what felt like eternity, as he absorbed the realization that Rob too felt the magnetic pull between them.

That he wasn't alone in the need.

The wanting.

His head was swimming with thoughts, questions, images, but he couldn't articulate any of them. He just sat there, frozen with surprise.

It was Rob who finally broke the spell, turning away abruptly with what sounded like a muttered curse.

"I need to check on Milo and Ovaltine."

He threw the words over his shoulder when he was already halfway to the door, and before Jonah could say anything, he was gone.

Still stunned, Jonah didn't move, although the sharp snap of the door closing made him jump.

Rob was attracted to him...

That thought racketed through his head, ping-ponging back and forth, trailed by others both collateral and random.

*I thought it was just me...*

*He wants to buy the clinic...*

*What would it be like...?*

Images of what it might be like to hold Rob, kiss him, make love with him invaded his mind, and he lost his ability to breathe.

*I couldn't...*

Yet, there was no mistaking the rush of heat that fired down his spine and straight into his groin.

Then one thought overrode all the others and drew him up short.

*Why did Rob leave so abruptly?*

*You'd think he'd want to talk things through a little...*

*Probably because you sat there gawking at him like a largemouth bass gasping on the riverbank...*

Galvanized by the realization he'd made no real reaction to anything Rob had said, probably sending the wrong message entirely, he sprang to his feet and headed to the isolation area.

Rob was back on the floor by the cage, using his stethoscope to listen to one of the pup's chests.

When he straightened and removed the earpieces, Jonah asked, "How are they doing?"

Easier to start there than to reopen the can of worms Rob had thrown at him.

Or maybe that should be cans, in the plural, even though there was one bigger than the others.

"They're holding their own, but I'm not terribly optimistic, despite the CPMA treatment," Rob replied, and Jonah appreciated the honesty, and the hint of sadness in Rob's tone. "I think it's going to be a long road for them, if they make it through the night."

"You're not planning to stay here with them all night, are you?"

He felt a little hypocritical asking the question that way. There'd been a number of nights when he'd slept in the clinic to monitor a patient.

"I haven't decided yet." Rob glanced up, then immediately looked back at the pups. "Would that be a problem?"

Jonah found himself shaking his head, although he really wanted Rob to go home and get some rest.

"No, but I can stay instead."

Rob shrugged. "It's no problem. They're my patients, so I'll stay. You go on home."

Besides that one glance, he'd kept his gaze lowered, and Jonah was suffused by the need to have him look up. Hopefully he could gauge what was going through his head by his expression.

He gathered his courage.

"Listen. You've thrown a lot of…ideas at me today." That brought Rob's head up, and Jonah found himself on the receiving end of a narrow-eyed stare. It almost dried up the words on his tongue, but he found the strength to forge ahead.

"The documentary. Your interest in buying the clinic…"

That was as far as he could go, whatever nerve he'd dredged up deserting him again.

Rob's lips twitched into a shadow of a smile.

"Not to mention suggesting that I want to sleep with you," he said, amusement and regret somehow both coming through in his voice and expressive face. "I'm usually more cautious about getting intimate with anyone," he confessed. "But I've been thinking about it since the moment I saw you, and it just…came out."

Would this man ever stop surprising him? Jonah was beginning to think not.

"It's okay," he muttered, not sure what else to say just then, mired in the kind of deep confusion he'd never experienced before.

"And it was ridiculous of me too," Rob continued, his voice a little bitter. "Considering you've been giving me the cold shoulder most of the day, it was stupid of me to think you might be interested in me in that way."

That rocked Jonah back on his heels, and he heard himself say, "No. No, it wasn't." Rob's eyes darkened, until all that was left was a ring of what looked like fire around his dilated pupils, and Jonah stepped back instinctively, knowing that if he didn't, he'd be lost. Fear and desire were at war within him, and, this time, fear won. "I… I just need time to think," he croaked, before turning around and fleeing.

Running from the intensity of his own desires.

# CHAPTER EIGHT

EVEN AFTER JONAH left the clinic, Rob's stress level stayed high, and he couldn't stop going over and over the conversation they'd had.

Jonah's obvious shock and hesitancy on hearing his confession, coupled with the other man's seeming admission that he too felt the attraction between them, had thrown him into a tailspin.

He wasn't normally so aggressive or forward. In fact, most of his relationships had been forged after the other man had made the first move. Rob could flirt with the best of them, but when it came to actually taking things to the next level, he tended to hang back, let the other person be vulnerable first.

Vulnerability.

That tended to be a hard one for him.

When he'd first started dating, there'd been some rejection involved. He'd assumed the other person was as into him as he was interested in them, and had been crushed when they turned out to only want sex—or not want him at all. And he'd never been the kind to give of himself—physically or emotionally—in a casual way. He was all or nothing.

Which made his approach to Jonah that much more unusual.

Sure, there'd been flashes, moments when he'd thought he'd seen an equal attraction in Jonah, but they'd been fleeting. Plus, he'd sensed a very real resistance from Jonah, as though even if he were interested in Rob, he didn't want to be.

Even hearing that Jonah only got involved in short-term, informal couplings or one-night stands should have been a turnoff, but actually wasn't.

Instead, it made him want to be the man who changed his attitude. Who made him want to keep coming back for more and more. Maybe never want to leave.

Which was another problem, since leaving Butler's Run was exactly what Jonah seemed determined to do. From what he'd said, only an aging golden retriever kept him from riding off into the sunset on a search for adventure.

They could simply switch places—Rob taking over Jonah's life and giving him his—and ostensibly they'd both be happy.

But Rob knew he wouldn't be happy. At least, not if that were to happen right now.

There really was unfinished business between them. At least in Rob's mind.

He'd never felt this way about anyone before—more than attracted, almost obsessed—and it was uncharted territory.

With a sigh, he checked on the puppies one more time, adjusting their drips, and set an alarm for three hours' time. Making his way to the staff lounge where there was an old couch, he found that Jonah had put out a pillow and a light blanket, and the concern warmed him. After toeing off his shoes, he stretched out and threw the cover over his legs. He knew he should try to doze, but he was still wired from his conversation with Jonah, so he opened his reading app on his phone and tried to concentrate on the thriller he'd been reading.

When his phone rang, his heart stumbled, until he realized it was Beeta.

He'd hoped it was Jonah, wanting to talk.

"Hey," he said, after clicking through to the call. "What's up?"

"That's what I'm calling to find out. I went by your room and you weren't there. Where are you?"

Beeta's rapid-fire questioning made him shake

his head. Anyone listening to them would think she was the older sibling.

"I'm at the clinic still. We had a pair of puppies come in with parvovirus. I'm monitoring them overnight."

"Are you getting paid for that?" While he wouldn't classify her as only concerned with money, she was a staunch advocate for everyone getting paid for whatever work they put in.

"That wasn't the arrangement, B, and I'm okay with it. No one asked me to stay. It was my decision."

The sound she made was one of irritation, but thankfully she didn't pursue that line of conversation. Instead, she asked, "Did your friend decide whether he wants to be a part of the documentary or not?"

"I'll find out in the morning." He'd completely forgotten about the documentary, with everything else going on. "He has a lot on his mind right now."

Probably the understatement of the decade, but the truth, nonetheless.

"At this point, I'm not sure I'm even going to bother with it."

"The documentary?"

"Yeah. They had us come all this way, assuring us everything was set, and now it's just one big hassle and delay. I'm fed up."

"At least give the council a chance to change their minds. As you said, we've come all this way…" And he definitely wasn't ready to leave.

She snorted, impatience fairly rolling off the sound. "I'm not going hat in hand. We were invited to be here, and they're being ridiculous. Even if they agree to allow us to film the Easter parade, I might still decide not to do the film. Then we can get back to civilization quicker than we planned."

Rob experienced an irrational annoyance at her characterization of Butler's Run as somehow outside the realm of civilization. For all her love of the outdoors, having lived in LA for years Beeta could be a snob about small towns, but her tone still irked him.

"You can leave," he said, deciding on the spur of the moment to break the news to her this way, rather than face-to-face, as he'd initially planned to. "But I'll be staying a while longer."

That silenced Beeta for a few seconds, but not for long.

"What do you mean? Why? What would you be staying for?"

"I like it here," he said, evenly, just as Gilligan

the cat wandered into the lounge and, without a pause, jumped onto the blanket over his legs.

"What's there to like?" Beeta couldn't contain her astonishment.

*Jonah Beaumont.*

But he kept that thought to himself.

"You know I've been looking for the right place to settle down—"

"You can't be serious. Besides, they already have a vet here. You'd compete with your friend?"

As though a part of the conversation, Gilligan found a comfortable spot and sat blinking at Rob, for all the world as if he were offering support.

"No. Jonah is thinking about selling his practice, and I'm thinking about buying it."

Once more, Beeta was reduced to silence. Gilligan climbed up onto Rob's chest and lay down, head butting him once, obviously demanding pets. When Rob obliged, the black cat started making biscuits on his shoulder.

"You're nuts," Beeta said frankly. "I think after two months you'll be climbing the walls because of the sameness. Moving here, after living in LA? Preposterous!"

It was on the tip of his tongue to remind her he'd only moved to LA because of her, but he bit that organ instead. He'd never come right out and said that to her, although both of them knew it was true. While he was off at school on his parents' dime, Beeta had been doing hard graft in coffee shops and retail stores, just to make enough money to live and go to college.

It hadn't been fair, and the guilt he'd felt had caused him to want to help her in whichever way he could. Well, he'd done that, and now it was time to get on with his life, but he didn't feel like having a long, protracted discussion with her about his plans.

"Maybe," he said, just to placate her. "But I'm going to give it a shot anyway."

"Good luck with it." She always retreated to sarcasm when unsure or hurt. "This place is as bad as Johnstown, and we both know how bad *that* was."

And he didn't bother to remind her that he actually liked the small town near where they grew up.

That would have just gotten her more riled up.

Gilligan headbutted him again, as though he'd read Rob's mind and agreed with him.

Jonah took Eunice out for her late evening walk, glad that it was a warm evening. The old dog suffered terribly with arthritis during the colder months, even with regular treatment for her joints and hip dysplasia. As the golden shuffled her way from bush to bush, Jonah looked back on the day just gone.

Had it only been one day? It felt longer, as though too much had happened and his brain couldn't reconcile the timeline being so short.

His head was also still spinning with the questions and concerns Rob had brought into his life. That man had definitely turned his world upside down.

"Be logical, Jonah," he said aloud, making Eunice lift her head and look at him with enquiring eyes. When he ruffled her ears, she went back to her nature investigations.

Yes. It made sense to cut through the noise and look at each of the issues separately. Logically. And do it in a logical order—easiest to hardest.

*Hardest...*

Just thinking that word made him snort, since he'd been in what felt like an almost constant state of erection since Rob came back into his life. The truncated laugh seemed to annoy Eunice, and she woofed at him in reprimand.

She liked her late-night strolls to be done in silence so she could hear the wind blowing and the wildlife noises. Being more than a little deaf meant any comments from Jonah were unwelcome.

"Sorry," he said, rubbing his hand down her back. "Just my juvenile sense of humor."

So, the easiest question was whether to participate in the documentary or not. On the plus side it might raise his professional profile, so that when he started looking for new opportunities, he had something extra to offer. Yet, that wasn't really enough of a reason to do it.

Did he really want or need a facsimile of the internet fame Rob enjoyed, and yet seemed to dislike, if not despise?

No.

And Rob wasn't terribly keen on doing this doc anyway.

*Doing this doc...*

This time he was able to keep his laughter to himself so as not to disturb Eunice, even though it rose like a hysterical bubble into his throat. But the double entendre almost made him abandon his train of thought and consider that Rob had, indeed, expressed a desire to do this particular doc.

*Stop it, Jonah. You're acting like a teenager.*

Dragging his mind out of the gutter, he brought it back on task.

Realistically, he had no idea whether his involvement would weigh the scale one way or another with the town council. But the bottom line was that Rob had asked for his help, and, no matter what else was happening between them, he owed the other man for stepping in at the clinic.

So, that was settled. He'd tell Rob that he'd be in the documentary.

Next was the suggestion he might want to eventually buy the practice.

It really should be a no-brainer. Rob had the credentials to be an asset to the clinic, and intimated he had the funds to buy it as well.

So why was Jonah hesitating there too? He should be firing off emails to his lawyer for advice, and figuring out exactly how to go about it, if Rob really was serious.

*Because it's Rob, and I'm burning inside for him. And if we sleep together, it'll complicate things. And if we don't, I might just spontaneously combust.*

That about summed it up, and made him realize he couldn't avoid the biggest of the questions: whether to make good on his near confession to Rob that he was attracted to him too and see where that all led.

Eunice had reached the end of her self-allotted distance and stood for a moment, looking up into the sky, before turning back toward the house. Jonah turned too and, for the first time in a long time, found himself really looking at his home.

He'd grown up here, after his father's far too early demise, which had brought him and his mother back to Butler's Run from Virginia, where his dad had been stationed.

Suddenly, he remembered the fear he'd felt on seeing the house, and his grandmother, for the first time. The car coming up the long driveway—the house was on five acres, he'd later learn, and set back far from the road—the big old oaks on either side seeming to reach out to grab at them. Then the elderly woman opening the door before they even got there.

Gran had been medium height and ramrod straight, salt-and-pepper hair pulled back into the neatest bun you'd ever see. Although she was stocky, there was nothing matronly about her. No one would expect Matilda Hawthorne to bake them cookies, or make a fuss if they fell. A pillar of the nearby Baptist church, where her own maternal grandfather had been a preacher, she was upright and forthright. And to him, just then, terrifying.

Even at just six years old, he'd recognized his mother's trepidation, and now realized he'd absorbed it from her.

*She's a dragon, Lonie. And she'll consume us if we move back there. Besides, she said she didn't want to have anything to do with me after I married Sam against her wishes.*

He'd heard them talking in the kitchen—Mom and Aunt Lonie—just a few months before. Although he was supposed to be in bed, how could he sleep when his auntie, who he adored, was visiting?

*You can't stay here alone, by yourself, Myra. Even with Sam's death benefit, how're you going to make ends meet? You need people around you that you can count on.*

Jonah had almost stepped into the room then, ready to shout that Momma wasn't alone. She had him, and could count on him too. He'd be good and take care of her, the way Daddy said he should whenever he left to go on deployment.

*You take care of your momma while I'm away, you hear?*

*I will, Daddy.*

And he had, hadn't he? He never gave her any trouble, although sometimes feelings he didn't understand boiled and boiled inside him, making him want to hit someone or something. Anyone. Anything. But he held all that inside, because he didn't want to make Mom cry any more than she already did.

So, he was ready to stand up to Aunt Lonie. Tell her to go away and leave them alone…

*You're right, Lonie. I can't stay here alone...*

It was the first time he'd realized he didn't count. Not really.

That he wasn't enough, couldn't be enough for the people he wanted to please the most.

Time and again he'd read between the lines of what others said and realized there must be something lacking in him—something that created emotional distance between him and those around him.

His mother, grandmother, even Aunt Lonie and Carmen.

It wasn't that he couldn't love, or wasn't prepared to make an effort for those he loved, but somehow that love and effort seemed insufficient.

And there, right there, was why he hesitated about getting involved with Rob.

Now though, he had to consider how he'd feel if he weren't enough for Rob. If the other man found him somehow deficient as a partner, either in work or in bed. Or both.

*But you don't plan to stick around, do you? You'll be leaving. So, why make this into a federal case? Things don't work out, you sell up and move on. No harm, no foul.*

It was only when Eunice gave a sigh and sat down that Jonah realized he'd been standing in the darkness of the night, unmoving, for what the dog probably thought was an unconscionable amount of time.

"Sorry, girl. Come on, let's go home."

But the house, although well-lit and infinitely familiar, suddenly seemed more like a jail than a home. Solitary confinement awaiting.

If you didn't count the four-legged companion slowly shuffling beside him along the path.

"You are more than enough for me, Eunice," he heard himself say, as if she'd understand him and needed the approbation. "You're the goodest girl ever, and I love you."

Funny how easy it was to love an animal, and both tell and show them so, and how hard it was to open himself up to another human being...

# CHAPTER NINE

AFTER A RESTLESS NIGHT, when he was back and forth keeping an eye on the puppies, Rob was just about to head back to the hotel to shower and change when Jonah got to work.

He didn't look any better rested than Rob felt.

"How're the babies?" Jonah asked, first thing.

"Made it through the night," Rob answered, stifling a yawn. "Still not out of the woods, but I'm a little bit more hopeful about them."

"Good. You go on and get outta here. Go get some rest." Rob was about to object, but Jonah held up his hand. "I know you probably dozed a bit, but that's not enough. Get some sleep and come in this afternoon, if you feel up to it. We can manage the workload, and although I'm sure you'd be okay working with little sleep, I'd prefer you be well rested."

Rob couldn't help grinning at the other man's workmanlike tone.

"Yes, boss." And he threw in a salute for good measure.

Jonah snorted, but his lips twitched into a smile nonetheless.

"Don't be a smart-ass."

"Can't help it," he replied, feeling somehow buoyed by the interaction. "Ask Beeta. She'll tell you."

"Oh, which reminds me… Tell your sister I'll take part in the documentary."

Rob felt his grin widen.

"Great. I'll let her know, but I have to warn you, she's pretty fed up with the whole thing at this point. Even if they give her permission to film the parade and horse show, she might decide to not go ahead with the shoot."

Jonah nodded slowly, his gaze fathomless.

"Don't make no never mind. If she decides to stay and film, I'm in. What about you?"

Genuinely confused, Rob asked, "What do you mean?"

Jonah cocked his head to one side, his habitual poker face firmly in place.

"If she decides not to do the film and leaves, are you going too?"

Surprised that he would even ask that, Rob stared at the other man, trying to figure out if he was serious. After their conversation last night, he'd have thought he'd know the answer to that question was a resounding no. Maybe he thought Rob had been joking, or had changed his mind? Did he really think he was that fickle or flaky?

Or was it some unwarranted lack of self-confidence making Jonah believe Rob didn't really want him, the way he'd said he did?

Unable to decide, and aware of other people moving around the clinic, all he could do was slowly—ever so slowly—shake his head.

"No, Jonah. I'm not going anywhere. Not until you and I get some stuff sorted out."

Something flashed behind those sleepy eyes but was quickly masked as Jonah gestured Rob toward his office, and Rob fell into step beside him to walk down the corridor.

"What will I have to do, if she goes ahead?" The change of subject wasn't lost on Rob, but he let it pass without comment.

"Once Beeta firms up the shoot, I'll go over the process with you," he told Jonah. "She goes for a conversational style of dialogue, so there's no script. All the excitement is provided by her camera angles and shots."

"Really?" Jonah asked, as he opened his office door. "What you do seemed pretty exciting to me."

"You watched some of the videos?" He knew

Jonah hadn't known about the docs before he'd come to town. Which meant he'd somehow, over the past couple of days, made time to check them out.

The thought gave Rob a pleasant jolt.

Jonah just shrugged, not making eye contact. "A few. They were interesting. Everyone had made such a fuss, I wanted to see for myself what all the hoopla was about."

Although he was obviously trying to sound casual, there was a defensive note to his voice that made Rob smile. He coughed to hide it and inadvertently made himself yawn.

"You're beat," Jonah said, giving him a stern glance. "Get outta here. I'll keep an eye on your babies. I'll see you when I see you."

"Not before I give my girlfriend some love," he replied, already stooping down beside Eunice's bed and ruffling the fur around her neck. "Right, girl? How dare he suggest I just ignore you?"

Eunice just sat there, taking his affection like the queen she was, and offering a small kiss as her official acceptance of his tribute.

But Jonah was right, Rob knew. He was exhausted. So, with a last hug, he let Eunice go and stood up.

"Okay, I'm outta here, as ordered." It amused

him to hear the way he'd unconsciously mimicked Jonah's Southern intonation. "I'll see you later."

"Yes, sir," came the answer, but, just as he'd gotten to the door, Jonah continued, "And if you're up for it, let's do dinner this evening, to discuss some of the other issues."

Rob froze with his hand on the knob, his heart suddenly pounding at a frantic pace. But when he turned to look at Jonah, the other man was seemingly focused on his computer screen.

Ironic, really, that Jonah had made the suggestion. During the long night just past, Rob had made the decision to bring up neither the purchase of the practice nor his physical interest in Jonah again. He'd seen the tension in Jonah and didn't want to exacerbate it.

"I'm guessing the venue won't be Lonie's?"

Jonah's gaze flicked up for an instant before those lazy, sexy eyelids drooped again, shielding the expression in his eyes.

"No. I have somewhere else in mind."

"Okay. Just let me know what time."

"Uh-huh."

Taking that as a dismissal, Rob exited the office, but he couldn't hold back a grin. And he was still smiling as he dialed Beeta's number to tell her that Jonah had agreed to do the documentary.

And the feeling of anticipation that had fired through him when he'd heard Jonah say he wanted to talk about "other issues" stayed with him, keeping him awake, tossing and turning, until exhaustion dragged him down into sleep.

A spring thunderstorm rolled in, bringing heavy rains and the threat of flooding. Although the weather people had been predicting it for the last couple of days, they'd underestimated the severity of it. The clinic had a slew of canceled appointments that afternoon, which turned out to be a good thing when, after a particularly violent clap of thunder, the lights went out. When they didn't come back on after ten minutes, Jonah called the power company and was told a substation had been damaged by lightning.

As for when it would be repaired and the power would come back on, they couldn't say.

"I'm sorry, folks," Jonah told the few people waiting before explaining what he'd been told. "We're going to have to reschedule. Until I know when the power's coming back on, I'm going to use the generator to keep the hospital area running. But please, wait until the lightning's moved off before you leave."

"Yeah," Tom Kingston said. "No use leaving 'cause of the dark and getting all lit up out there."

Jonah was still chuckling as he made his way to the back of the clinic to tell the staff to get ready to go home, once the storm eased up.

"There aren't a lot of animals in the hospital," he replied to Alan, when the youngster asked if he should stay to feed the animals as usual later in the afternoon. "I'm gonna hang around, so I'll do it."

When the worst of the lightning passed, the clients left, followed not too long after by the staff. Jonah put on a raincoat and trotted out to the shed where the generator was housed and got it going. At some point it would be nice to upgrade to an automatic unit, he thought, as he sprinted back to the clinic building, trying avoid the next shower, which he could see coming in the distance. But maybe it would be easier to let the next owner take care of that, if they wanted to.

After all, when he'd bought into the practice initially, Doc Harding didn't even have a generator in place. Jonah had only been able to convince the old guy to install one after they'd been shut down for close to a week after a hurricane passed through.

He was hanging up his raincoat when he heard the front door open and Rob call out.

"Back here," he said, wishing his heart wouldn't start galloping like a colt seeing pasture for the first time every time the darn man was close by.

"What's going on?" Rob was damp, his shirt sticking to his chest, so that when he raised his hands to slick the droplets of water off his hair, every muscle was delineated.

Jonah looked away, but the image seemed seared onto his retinas.

"Storm knocked out a substation, so I closed for the day." He moved to the sink to wash his hands, keeping Rob out of his line of sight. "Even though the generator can run most of the clinic, I don't want to overtax it by using anything like the X-ray machine, or the autoclave. Besides, it's a blessing in disguise for the staff, you know? They've been putting in extra hours to keep up, without complaint, and it'll do 'em good to get some unexpected time off."

Rob moved toward the isolation area, asking, "How're the babies?"

"They're still with us. Lethargic, and not interested in food, so still on the drip. I did get them to take a little oral rehydration though."

"I'll call and update the owner," he said, as he disappeared to look in on his babies.

"He called earlier, and I spoke to him. Told him we'd give him a call tomorrow morning to update again."

"Oh, great." His voice floated out from the other room. "Hey, did someone clean these babies up?"

"Yep. Alan is as obsessed with them as you are. He wouldn't leave until he'd made sure they were clean and comfortable. Insisted on trying them with a little more rehydration fluid too."

"He's a really reliable worker. Do you think he'll go to school to become a tech?"

Jonah pondered that for a second and then shrugged, forgetting that Rob couldn't see him.

"I don't know. He has time to figure it out. He's successful here because everyone knows and understands his quirks are caused by his Asperger's. His mother tends to be a bit…over-protective. It's going to be up to Alan to decide whether he wants to go on to college or not."

"That's one of the benefits of growing up in a small town where everyone knows you." Rob's voice came from almost right behind him, making Jonah stiffen. "Even though it can be a pain too, when you need some understanding you're more likely to get it."

"Hmm." He didn't have a reply; he was too busy concentrating on not looking at the other man. Every inch of skin on his back was prickling with awareness, heat traveling through nerve endings to make his entire body feel supersensitive.

"Did you like growing up here?"

Jonah moved away as slowly as he could, although it was the last thing he wanted to do.

If he didn't, he wouldn't be able to carry on a coherent conversation. Even so, Rob's scent, warm and fresh, seemed to follow him.

Busying himself with collecting some soiled drapes from a receptacle, he replied, "Not at first, but it grew on me, over time."

Rob had moved to another receptacle and was gathering up the bag there. "You weren't born here?"

"Nope. I was born in Virginia. Mom and I moved back here after Daddy died. I was six, and terrified of my grandmother, who I'd never met before."

"Wow. You were six before you met her?"

"Yeah. Apparently, she didn't approve of my mom marrying my father. Grandma came from a pretty affluent background—you know, Black cotillion, mainstay of society, that type of thing—and Daddy was from the other side of the tracks. She'd raised Mom to follow in her footsteps. Even sent her to France to a finishing

school. So when Mom met Daddy at college—
just a guy there on scholarship—and decided to
marry him, Grandma disowned her."

"Wow. That's hardcore."

"You know it." They both shook their heads in
disbelief, as Jonah went on, "When Daddy died,
Mom was going to stay in Virginia, although it
was too expensive for her to make ends meet.
Then Aunt Lonie came and told her Grandma
was offering her the opportunity to come back
here. I think she was reluctant to come back…"
Once more the conversation overheard so very
long ago came back to him, and he snorted. "Actually, I know she didn't really want to come
back. She called Grandma a dragon."

They were moving side by side toward the
mudroom, where the washer and dryer were lo-
cated, but both paused in unison just outside the
door. Jonah knew Rob was looking at him, and
he turned so they were face-to-face, but sepa-
rated by the bags of laundry.

"So, how bad did she turn out to be?"

There was true concern on Rob's face, as
though he dreaded hearing what was going to
come next, but Jonah shook his head, wishing
his hands were free so he could touch the other
man.

"Not bad, at all. I don't think Mom would have

stayed if Grandma had been abusive in any way, no matter how badly off we were financially. Grandma was tough, stern and strict, but we got along okay. She was even the one who fostered my interest in animals."

There was no mistaking the relief that crossed Rob's expression.

"I'm glad to hear that."

"Mothers and daughters are a different dynamic than grandmothers and grandkids, I think. Mom and Grandma still bucked heads occasionally over the years, but by then it was more of a generational gap than the old arguments."

Realizing they were just standing there with the laundry in their hands, Jonah moved ahead of Rob into the mudroom and dropped the bag on the ground.

"She was old-fashioned, and old-school in a lot of ways. You kept your private business to yourself and presented a respectable, God-fearing front to the world, no matter what was going on behind the scenes."

Rob looked up from where he was loading the machine, his gaze searching.

"I'm guessing your being gay didn't go over so well with her. Did that cause a rift?"

Jonah leaned a hip against the dryer and tried to smile, although it felt stiff and false on his face.

"It might sound cowardly, but I waited until she'd passed to come out. She had cancer, and didn't have much longer to live by the time I'd sorted my sexuality out in my head, you know? I knew how she'd feel about it, from things that she'd said about gay people, that there was something fundamentally wrong with them. She was so old-school, and I just didn't want to disappoint or hurt her."

Rob straightened and reached for the detergent.

"I don't think it's cowardly at all. In fact, it's kind of loving, in a way. Why potentially make her worry about you, and cause her last days to be unhappy?" A flash of what looked like pain crossed his face, as he continued, "That was my plan too, with my *abuela*, and I've always wished it had worked out, but it didn't."

"What happened?"

Rob didn't answer immediately, just measured the soap into the machine and closed the lid with a snap. Then he turned to face Jonah, and he was frowning. That was such an unusual occurrence, Jonah found himself focusing on the conversation with even greater attention.

"I got outed, by a guy at school." He shook his head, gaze taking on a distant look, as though seeing it all over again. "It was my own fault. Other kids said they thought he was gay, I thought he was flirting with me, and I'd had a crush on him for a while. So, I took the chance and tried to kiss him."

"Uh-oh."

"Yeah." Now a small, rueful smile replaced the frown. "That led to a fight, which had us ending up in the principal's office, where it all came out—including me—in front of my parents."

Despite the other man's smile, which wasn't that convincing anyway, Jonah ached for the young Rob, caught up in such a situation.

"How did your parents take it?"

He shrugged slightly, tilting his head from side to side. "My parents are decent people, and even if they'd been tempted to disown me, they didn't. Papa, in particular, had some trouble with it, but eventually he got over it. But my *abuela*... Nah, man, she was horrified. Was sure I was going to hell, praying over me, crying, the whole nine yards. That made me so sad, and angry."

"I'm sorry, man. That's terrible."

"Don't feel bad," he replied, that crooked smile tipping his lips again. "It was a long time ago, and I didn't mention it for sympathy, just to let you know that I completely understand how you felt about not telling your grandmother you were gay."

"Thanks for that," Jonah replied, meaning it sincerely. He'd secretly viewed his actions back then just as he'd told Rob—as cowardice. But now, having heard Rob's perspective and the outcome of his story, maybe someday he could put it to rest without that burden of guilt.

His grandmother really would have been unhappy, knowing her grandson was gay. Thank goodness neither his mother nor Aunt Lonie had seemed to care. That had been a blessing.

Rob brushed his hands together, as though to dislodge the last of their conversation.

"What else do you have to do around here? You might as well make use of me while you have me."

"Sure. I made a list of things I was planning to do this afternoon, once I decided to close the clinic. It's kinda nice to be able to do them at a more leisurely pace, rather than have to fit them in between patients. If you could fill the autoclave, that would be great. When the power comes back on, I'll start it."

"You got it, boss," he replied with one of his salutes, which always made Jonah want to laugh.

And Jonah found himself still smiling as he

went about cleaning and inventorying the clinic, listening to Rob whistling in the distance, just happy to have the other man there.

# CHAPTER TEN

JONAH WAS IN his office, trying to sort through the paperwork on his desk, when Rob stuck his head around the door to say, "Beeta's on her way here."

"Did she say what happened at the meeting?"

Rob came closer, shaking his head, a thoughtful expression on his face.

"Nope, and I can't figure out what that means. It could be that she's planning to go ahead and wants to discuss the schedule with both of us, or that she wants to tell us face-to-face it's not happening."

The slow *thump-thump-thump* of Eunice's tail on the floor drew Rob like a magnet as usual, but this time he simply sat on the floor, cross-legged, so as to be able to drape an arm across her neck to pat her.

"Which one seems more likely to you?"

"Probably...she's pulling the plug. She sounded pretty fed up when she called."

Jonah's heart skipped a beat. Although Rob had said he was going to stay whether the documentary got made or not, Jonah wasn't sure he believed him. Even though he was right there, sitting on the floor petting Eunice, the thought of him somehow remaining a part of their lives in Butler's Run seemed absurd.

"And, what about you?"

Rob looked up at him, not smiling but with eyes gleaming coppery, and something about his expression hinted at amusement.

"What about me? I already told you I'm not going until we sort some things out, and you've told me you need time to think. So, I'm staying."

"How long?"

Now the amusement faded, leaving Rob's expression watchful.

"I don't know. How long do you need to think about everything?"

Jonah didn't answer, whatever he was contemplating replying fading away at the look in Rob's eyes—questioning, impatient.

Longing.

Was that longing for him, or for the fantasy small-town life Rob seemed determined to have?

Before either of them could say anything more, there was a banging on the front door, which made Eunice bark and struggle to get up.

"I'll get it," Jonah said, while Rob tried to calm the dog down.

Thankful for the reprieve, he hurried through the waiting area to unlock the door for the woman standing outside.

"Hi," she said, as he opened the door for her. "Thanks."

"You must be Beeta," he said, as he relocked the door behind her. The resemblance to Rob was marked—especially the eyes, although hers were a little darker. "I'm Jonah."

"Nice to finally meet you." Beeta smiled and stuck out her hand. "I met your Aunt Lonie this afternoon. If I didn't know better, I'd think she was planning to adopt that lunkhead of a brother of mine. She couldn't stop talking about him."

Jonah laughed, amused and yet wondering just what else Lonie might have said.

"Come on through to the office."

He noticed her looking around as they walked, pausing to glance into the reception area and through an open door into one of the examination rooms. No doubt trying to figure out what it was, exactly, her brother was thinking of getting himself into.

But she didn't ask any questions, or fill the silence with small talk. Instead, she strode alongside him with quick, long steps.

When Jonah stepped back to allow her to go through the office door ahead of him, she shot him a cheeky, sideways smile that reminded him so much of Rob, his breath hitched.

"Hey, sis. Forgive me for not getting up, but my girlfriend and I are having a moment."

"Hello, sweetie," Beeta said, going straight toward Eunice and offering a hand for sniffing. "You should be more careful about the company you keep. Nice girls like you don't need guys like this."

"Says you. Eunice knows I love her, and that's all there is to say about it."

"I'd have thought she'd have better taste," Beeta rebutted, as she bent to kiss the top of Rob's head. Then she tossed her bag onto a chair and sank down beside her brother on the floor, despite her chic ensemble. "What a day..."

Jonah retook his seat behind the desk, watching the byplay between the siblings. There was a high level of familiarity and comfort between them. Clearly, they knew each other extremely well.

"So, what's the verdict?"

Beeta scrunched up her nose. "The council agreed to a permit, of sorts. But it's so restrictive, I'd have a hell of a time getting any decent shots. I guess the person who didn't want the documentary made at all went around and convinced a bunch of people to sign a petition saying they didn't want their likeness, home or business in the film. Honoring their requests would hamstring me."

"Calling it off then?"

Beeta blew out a long breath and reached across Rob to pat Eunice.

"Yeah, I'm done. I told the Marsh Tacky folks, and they're upset but that can't be helped. I'm sending Gary and Lena home, then going to head up to Charleston for a few days before I go back to LA." She leaned back to give Rob an intent look. "What about you? Want to come to Charleston with me?"

"Nope." At Rob's reply, Jonah found himself releasing a breath he hadn't even realized he'd been holding. "I'm going to stick around here, like I told you."

Beeta suddenly turned her head to look straight at Jonah, and something about the quality of that look made him wonder what she was thinking.

"Well, if you change your mind, I won't be leaving until tomorrow." Looking from Rob to Jonah and back again, she added, "Why don't the three of us have dinner together this evening? I'd like to get to know Jonah a little better."

"Nope," Rob said again, giving his sister a smile that didn't quite seem to reach his eyes. "We already made plans to discuss the potential of my getting further involved with the practice, and since you've changed the timeline, that talk is even more important."

His answer seemed to shock Beeta, who stared at Rob for a few long seconds, before abruptly getting up.

"Well, okay, then." There was a sour note to her voice, although she too smiled. "I'll be heading back to the hotel to pack and let the rest of the team know what's happening." She looked at Jonah then, and shook her head slightly. "If I don't see you again before I leave, it was nice meeting you."

Rob got up too.

"I'll walk you out."

Between the headshake and her abrupt departure, Jonah was left once more wondering what she was thinking. Clearly, she was annoyed about Rob refusing to go to dinner or to Charleston with her, which made him recall that Rob had said his sister knew he had a hard time refusing her anything.

What had made him take such a hard line with her this time?

Maybe he didn't want Jonah spending time with his sister for some reason?

His cell phone rang just then, breaking him out of his reverie, and a glance showed it was Marnie Rutherford. With his heart in throat— hoping she wasn't calling to say another of her horses was ill—Jonah answered.

"Hi, Jonah," Marnie said when he'd answered. "Sorry to bother you, but I'm here in town and saw a young woman with a kitten she said she'd found outside her workplace. It looks to be in a pretty bad way, so I sent her to your clinic. She should be there any minute."

"Okay." His sense of relief was immediate, and he didn't bother to tell Marnie that the clinic was closed. He'd gladly do whatever he could for the kitten. "I'll look out for her."

"Thanks. Appreciate it. Talk to you soon."

Getting up, he moved down the hallway to- ward the front of the clinic, realizing as he got closer that Rob and Beeta were obviously still there, talking. The door to the waiting area was open and the voices carried through to him clearly.

"I know you, Rob. You'll get bored in a couple of months and that'll be that, unless you've al- ready locked yourself into something you can't get out of. How on earth can you even think you'll be happy here after living in LA? That's nuts."

"Maybe you don't really understand—"

Jonah came through the door, making sure to make as much noise as possible, to let them know he was there. He already felt bad about hearing what he had, but it had been unavoidable.

"I have a client coming in," he said, not breaking stride as he went past the siblings, who were standing in the middle of the waiting area.

"I thought you were closed?" Beeta said, her aggression evident.

"Doesn't matter," said Rob, before Jonah could reply. "If Jonah's willing to see the patient, that's his business."

"The person who sent her didn't know we were closed, and I don't mind taking a look at the kitten she found."

But he was feeling a little guilty about potentially causing a rift between Rob and his sister. They seemed so close, and Rob had said family was everything.

As he got to the front door, he saw a car driving up to the building. After unlocking the door, he stepped outside, allowing it to swing closed behind him and giving Rob and Beeta some privacy.

The woman who got out of the car was a stranger, and he watched as she walked toward him, a small box in her hands.

"Hi," she said, as she got within earshot. "Are you Dr. Beaumont?"

"Yes. I hear you found a little baby outside your work and it needs some help?"

"Yes," she said, shifting the box to under one arm so she could shake his hand, adding, "Amanda Parr," by way of introduction. "I found him just under my car. And when I went to pick him up, he hardly moved. I don't know what's going on with him."

"Come on in," he said, taking the box from her and looking into it. A ginger kitten, lying unmoving on a towel, looked back at him with dull eyes.

Just as they got to the door, it was pushed open from inside, and Beeta stepped out.

"What you got there, Jonah?" she asked, pausing to peer into the box. "Aww, just a baby. Make him better, okay?"

"I'll do my best," he replied, as he moved into the clinic, glad to see she seemed to be in a better mood.

With a wave, she let the door close behind them, and Rob was there peering into the box as he walked alongside Jonah.

"Tiny guy," was his only comment.

"Yeah. Can you take him into exam room one, while I go get my computer?"

"Sure."

Rob took the box from him, and Jonah headed for his office. While he gathered up his computer, Jonah thought back to what he'd heard Beeta say to Rob about his getting bored and not staying in Butler's Run.

It made perfect sense to him. In fact, he'd thought the same thing many times.

Butler's Run on a permanent basis after living in LA and traveling all over the country?

Ridiculous.

It was then the realization suddenly hit Jonah. He'd been tying himself up into knots over Rob, worried about the ramifications of getting involved with him professionally and personally, while the person who knew him best had already realized nothing would come of any of it. If Beeta was so sure that Rob wouldn't stick around, then there was nothing to worry about.

They could work together for a while, sleep together for a while, and then Rob would change his mind about settling down in Butler's Run and that would be that.

Sure, Jonah would have to find a new purchaser for the clinic, but he'd cross that creek when he came to it.

In the meantime, he could take a chance on enjoying the other man.

Why look a gift horse in the mouth?

# CHAPTER ELEVEN

THANKFULLY THE POWER came back on before they were ready to leave the clinic after five thirty, and Rob asked Jonah where he wanted to meet up for dinner.

"The restaurant is east of here, closer to my house than the hotel," Jonah replied. "So why don't you drive over to my place, and we'll drive there together?"

"Sure," he replied, both surprised and pleased, since he'd wondered about Jonah's home and was curious to see it.

After getting directions, he headed back to the hotel to change out of his scrubs and into more appropriate clothing.

Although, standing in front of the hotel closet, he wondered what that was, exactly. It wasn't a date; should he dress as though it were? Certainly he wanted to make a good impression on Jonah, show the other man his best side, so to speak. Yet, he didn't want to look as though he was trying too hard either. None of the LA styling that he'd had to wear in the past seemed right.

Finally, aware of time ticking away, he went with a black Henley and jeans, his favorite black boots and a turquoise pendant on a leather thong—a gift from his mother the previous Christmas. Hair loose, or back? Laughing at himself, he left the thick strands loose, but out of habit tucked a hair tie into his pocket.

Wallet, watch and a last look in the mirror, and he was out the door.

But before he closed it behind himself, he hurried back inside to spritz himself with cologne.

Nothing wrong with smelling nice!

Getting into the car, he acknowledged his anxiety about the evening ahead. Not even Beeta could understand how much this opportunity meant to him. Or, more accurately, she refused to believe he was serious, because it didn't suit her own agenda. At the end of their conversation earlier, she'd admitted as much.

"I can't imagine not having you close by," she'd finally said. "Not after all we've done together. You can open a clinic in LA, or nearby. Be closer to the family. Also," she'd added, as if unable to stop herself, "we can keep doing some videos together. Not all the time, like we have been, but every now and then."

Normally he appreciated her focused determination, her wish to keep her favorite brother close by, but not today.

Today it felt intrusive and overbearing.

Rob sighed, taking a hand off the wheel to rub at the back of his neck where an ache had settled.

Not that he totally blamed her for being concerned. Everything had happened so quickly, he sometimes wondered what had gotten into him too. But, on the other hand, he was an adult. Her older brother, to boot. The one who'd always looked out for her as best he could, while also letting her live her life the way she wanted.

Couldn't she at least acknowledge he had the right to do the same?

He'd been following the directions on his GPS, and now realized he must be close to his destination. Taking the indicated left turn, he found himself on a gravel road lined with old oak trees dripping with Spanish moss. It was only as he drove around a curve that he realized it wasn't a road, but a driveway leading to a large white two-story house.

Just as he was wondering if he'd made a wrong turn, the front door opened, and Jonah stepped out onto the wraparound porch.

"Good grief," Rob muttered, still taking in the old-world charm of the building. As soon as he got out, he called to Jonah, "This is where you live?"

With amusement in his voice, Jonah called back, "Yep. Like it?"

"It's amazing. Kinda big for just you and Eunice though, isn't it? Unless you have an entire family stashed in there somewhere."

"Nope. Just us two." They met at the bottom of the stairs and stood side by side, looking up at the facade. "It's a family place, so although I use maybe four rooms total, I can't bring myself to sell it."

"I'd beat you myself if you ever tried to. She's a grand Southern lady."

He turned his head just in time to see Jonah smile at him, and something about that curl of his lips made Rob's heart skip a beat.

"I'm too hungry to give you the tour now, but maybe when we get back?"

"I'd like that," he replied, wondering if he was imagining a shift in Jonah's demeanor. A lifting of his usual reticence. He seemed more relaxed.

"Great. Let me just lock up and we'll be on our way."

The drive to the restaurant took about fifteen minutes, and during that time, they spoke casually about the clinic and the untimely demise of Beeta's project.

"She's artistically spoiled," Rob said. "She's so used to getting her way, or doing her own thing, she doesn't like being given boundaries on her work. Hopefully she'll eventually get over herself, or she'll be butting heads with clients going forward."

Jonah sent him a sideways glance and seemed to hesitate for a moment before saying, "You once said you have a hard time saying no to her. Is there a reason, other than she's your sister?"

The question took him by surprise, but, after a moment, he didn't see any reason not to be honest.

"Yeah, there is. Beeta is the youngest—there are four of us—and closest to me in age. We've always been tight. And she's the only one my father refused to help with college. For some reason he decided that being a videographer was a ridiculous career path, and Beeta, being Beeta, got angry and left home right after graduating high school. She was in LA, working, trying to get through school when I graduated, so I moved there to help her finish."

"This might be a rude question, but why?"

Confused, Rob asked, "Why what?"

"Why did you think it was your job to help her through school?"

Rob felt a spurt of annoyance but swallowed it. After all, to an outsider it would be a reasonable question.

"You know how expensive UC Davis is, and I was only on partial scholarship. My parents shelled out a lot of money to help me get through vet school, while Beeta was struggling alone. Why wouldn't I want to help her out when I could? She's my sister."

"I guess," Jonah said. "But I have to say I admire you for putting your sister's needs ahead of your own ambitions—unless, of course, LA was your idea of a great place to live?"

"It wasn't and isn't." He hadn't meant to sound so emphatic, but he couldn't help the forceful way the words came out. "I've always wanted to live in a more rural setting, not having to budget an extra hour or two just to get from one place to the next, and deal with people who seem to have their heads in the clouds most of the time."

Jonah put on his indicator and turned into a parking lot that was about half-full of vehicles. When he'd parked, he turned off the ignition and turned in his seat to face Rob as he was reaching for the door handle. He was smiling and, beneath those sleepy lids, his eyes were glittering.

"Well, here you'll still have to drive a ways to get out to some of the farms, and unfortunately you can't cure stupid, which exists everywhere. But for the most part the people are down-to-earth, so we've got LA beat in that respect."

He'd spoken quietly, intimately, and although the words were humorous—even prosaic—Rob felt as if the temperature in the vehicle had gone up by twenty degrees. Unable to stop staring at Jonah's mouth, the urge to lean forward and capture those smiling lips with his own was almost overwhelming.

The distance between them narrowed, narrowed, until he could feel each rush of Jonah's exhales across his face, smell the mint on his breath, mixed with the warm scent of his cologne.

Heart hammering, Rob held his breath, about to close those last few inches...

Jonah inhaled sharply and popped the door handle, opening his door.

"Let's go get something to eat. I'm starving."

Squashing his disappointment, Rob replied, "Me too."

And he didn't try to hide the irony, which made Jonah send him a laughing look from those sexy, heavy-lidded eyes.

Inside, they were taken to a table overlooking

a salt marsh inlet, which was bathed in the last orange and rose tinges of the setting sun, with boats parked along a small dock. The vista was gorgeous and calming, and Rob allowed the lingering sexual tension to dissipate.

He'd made the decision not to push Jonah, and he'd stick to that, no matter how crazy the other man made him.

Instead of sitting across the table from Rob, Jonah chose the seat next to him, probably so he too could enjoy the view.

Once they'd placed their drink orders, Jonah got right down to business.

"I've been thinking it over, and I need to contact my business lawyer for advice, but what I propose is that we agree to a trial period where you work at the clinic for a salary. While that's happening, we can get all necessary legal details and contracts sorted out. It'll give us both an opportunity to figure out what, exactly, we want to do and when, long-term."

Was it ridiculous to feel impatient with this cautious approach?

"When you say a trial period, what are you thinking?"

"Two, maybe three months." Before Rob could say anything, he continued, "It'll take at least that long for the lawyer to figure out the legalities anyway. You know how slow they can be."

It felt like talking to Beeta all over again, but Rob knew he was being unfair to Jonah. And selfish too, if he were being honest with himself. Just because he'd made up his mind about what he wanted to do didn't mean that everyone else had to fall into line.

"Okay," he said, albeit reluctantly. "But I have to tell you I won't change my mind about this, unless something completely untoward happens."

Jonah's eyebrows rose at that, but he didn't ask for clarification. Instead, he said, "We can discuss the financial aspect of it more tomorrow. I never discuss money on an empty stomach."

Rob grunted, still annoyed but even more amused by that pronouncement.

The waiter brought their drinks, and they asked for a bit more time to order, since neither had looked at the menu. Once the waiter left the table again, Rob wondered if Jonah would go back to their discussion, but when next he spoke, the other man asked a question that came out of left field.

"What do you like, in bed?"

It was the last thing he'd expected, and the easy, casual way Jonah asked was shocking. No doubt that showed on his face, because Jonah snorted—a truncated laugh that surprised Rob even more.

"Why do you look like a deer caught in an illegal hunter's spotlight?" Jonah asked, amusement rife in his drawled question. "I'm curious. Besides, we're kinda negotiating here, aren't we? I'd like to know what I'm getting into."

It suddenly struck Rob that their past dealings, with Jonah playing his cards so close to his chest, and Rob doing the pursuing, had made him forget what Jonah's love life had been up to this point. He most likely had far more experience with these kinds of situations than Rob did, with a lot more "negotiations" under his belt.

For an instant it made Rob feel off balance. Even a little silly. But then he rallied.

"Afraid I might be into some kinky stuff?" he drawled in return, using the voice he did when he was trying to get a rise out of one of his siblings.

Jonah's lips twisted, and his eyelids drooped.

"Maybe," he said. "Forewarned is forearmed."

Jonah watched the various emotions play across Rob's face and enjoyed the show. Shock morphed to surprise, then faded to a narrow-eyed look of concentration. Jonah didn't look away, but held the other man's intent stare until Rob was the one to drop his eyes.

He'd never seen Rob thrown off balance, and felt something akin to pride that he'd been able to do it. This sexy Latin man was far too sure of himself, far too smooth to be allowed to always run the show. And to this point, Jonah realized he'd let him do just that.

He wasn't a pushover. Never had been. In fact, he'd always been the one in control of his own affairs—both businesswise and in his private life, such as it was.

But his reactions to Rob—so primitive and visceral—were a warning that he might not be able to control what was happening between them. Not completely anyway.

The best he could do was put the other man on notice that he'd do his utmost not to get in over his head by allowing Rob to set the pace or make all the decisions.

Finally, Rob looked up at him again and smiled one of his sly, cheeky smiles, but his eyes were wary.

"What do you want to know? I've never been asked that before. Usually, I just go with the flow, let things evolve naturally, without too much preplanning."

Jonah tilted his head, wondering what had created that cautious expression.

"Does talking about this make you uncomfortable?" he asked, now surprised at the tenderness he felt. "That wasn't my intention."

Shaking his head, a more natural smile breaking over his face, Rob said, "Not uncomfortable, really. It just feels strange to—how did you put it?—'negotiate' in this way."

"In the scene, I have to be careful not to put myself into situations I'm not prepared for," Jonah explained. "Sometimes men want more than I'm prepared to give, and it can turn dangerous."

Rob's face tightened. "Have you been hurt?"

The harshness of his tone came as a surprise, and Jonah jerked in his seat.

"No. Not recently, and not in the way you think, mainly because I've learned to ask questions up front."

Rob took a sip of his beer, almost as though buying time, his gaze never leaving Jonah's. When he put down the glass, his face was somber.

"Tell me who hurt you, and how, and I'll promise never, ever to do what they did."

Jonah waved his hand, trying to dismiss this strange turn the conversation had taken, even as his heart beat so heavily he could hear it in his ears.

How had this gone from what he'd thought of as a simple exploratory chat to this? And why did it make him almost feel like crying to hear Rob say those words?

"Forget about that," he said, even though a part of him wanted to tell Rob that old story— one he'd never shared with anyone. "It's long gone. Dust in the wind. This is about you. Don't turn it back on me."

Rob shook his head. "One day I'll get it out of you," he said, making it a promise and a threat, all rolled into one.

"But not tonight," Jonah replied, wanting to kiss Rob so badly his face hurt. "Tonight, I just need to know what you like. What you want."

Rob's lips parted, and he started to speak, then stopped, as if rethinking what he'd been about to say. Then he shook his head again, as though in disbelief, and replied, "I like a little excitement in the bedroom, but not BDSM or anything like that. I've experimented some, and had fun, but I've also had completely vanilla relationships and enjoyed them too. If that's what you want, I'm good with it."

*Vanilla.*

Was he vanilla? Jonah had always sort of

thought so, since his need for control made it harder to experiment in many ways. Who could he trust to experiment with? But now, looking across the table at Rob, he couldn't decide.

Around Rob he felt anything but vanilla, which was synonymous with ordinary. Boring.

It was time to find out exactly what he was, and get some relief from this constant thrum of desire.

"I think we'll need to figure out if that's really what I want," he said, his voice coming out like a truck driving over gravel. "How about we get started later?"

And the flare of Rob's gaze, which darkened almost to black in a blink, was all the answer he needed.

# CHAPTER TWELVE

THE WAITER CAME back just then, and Rob placed an order for the first entrée that caught his eye, pretty damn sure he wouldn't be able to eat anyway. And even if he could, he doubted he'd taste anything.

He was still reeling from the turn the conversation with Jonah had taken, his emotions ping-ponging between embarrassment and excitement.

It was interesting, and somewhat disconcerting, to know Jonah had had such a varied sex life in comparison to his. Rob wasn't an innocent. Not in the slightest. But obviously Jonah was leagues ahead of him when it came to experience.

Knowing that didn't bother him, and now that they'd had this conversation, he could see the benefit of it. Why stumble forward into intimacy, when just talking it out could save you from making hurtful mistakes?

Pushing everything else aside, he leaned a little closer to Jonah and said, "I want to tell you something. Something you should know about me."

Jonah turned an inquiring look his way, over the rim of his glass, and raised his eyebrows.

"The truth is, I just want to know what will drive you wild, give you maximum satisfaction. That's where I get the most pleasure."

Jonah's eyes widened, and the flare of desire in them almost incinerated Rob right then and there.

"We'll have to discuss that further," Jonah murmured in that gravelly tone that sent shivers down Rob's spine.

The waiter approached with their meal, and Rob was happy to see he'd apparently ordered a pork chop, mashed potatoes and steamed vegetables. He wasn't a fussy eater, but it was disconcerting to realize he couldn't remember ordering because of the turn the conversation had taken.

After placing their plates in front of them, the waiter hesitated long enough that Rob looked up at him inquiringly.

"Excuse me," the young man said. "But I have to ask. Are you Vet Vic?"

From the corner of his eye, he saw Jonah lift

his head to stare at the waiter. Rob feigned confusion, as he asked, "Sorry, who?"

"Oh." The young man's face fell into lines of disappointment. "Never mind. Sorry to bother you."

After he'd walked away, Jonah asked, "Why'd you do that?"

"Couple of reasons," he replied, ignoring his dinner and making sure Jonah was paying attention. "Firstly, with the documentary falling through, and my decision that it would have been my last one, Vet Vic is officially dead."

"Okay." Those sleepy eyes were intent on his, and Rob couldn't help leaning just a little closer.

"Secondly, and most importantly, I'm out with you. I don't want anyone making a fuss. I just want to enjoy being with you."

Jonah looked away, but Rob noticed the upward tilt of his lips and was happy with that.

After eating in silence for a little while, Jonah once more surprised Rob by going off in a completely different conversational tack. "Did your grandmother ever accept your gayness?"

Rob felt a pang of remembered hurt.

"I don't think so, although she never brought it up. She was a worrier—always had been—and I think it was one more thing she worried about, though she never talked about it after that one time."

"She lived with you?"

It felt good to know Jonah was interested in his life, so Rob was smiling when he replied, "Yes. I never knew my *abuelo*—he died before I was born—but Abuela was there in my first memories. Mama worked alongside Papa on the ranch, and Abuela looked after the house and us. We used to drive her crazy, because she was sure we were going to kill ourselves every time we went outside."

Jonah chuckled. "My grandma was the opposite. She'd take Carmen and me to her friends' farms and let us run wild. I remember trying to ride one of the goats while she stood outside the pen laughing. You'd never think it to look at her, either. She was prim and proper, always dressed to the nines, but said little kids should get messy and have bumps and bruises."

"Meanwhile, my *abuela* was running after us, shouting, 'Put on your shoes!' 'Don't go in the mud!' 'Don't go near the pens with the bulls!' And was freaked out when we didn't listen."

Jonah laughed, and Rob loved the way the sound echoed in his chest. Jonah didn't laugh often enough.

"That must have been hard on both her and you kids too."

"It was, and of course we couldn't understand why she was that way. It was only after I got older that I thought to ask Mama if she knew why Abuela worried so much, and she explained that it was because of the things that happened when she was young. How her father had gambled away what they had, and they ended up living in a tent and working in the fields. Before that the children were going to school, had enough to eat and lived in a house. Then suddenly it was all gone.

"Mama said one of Abuela's brothers died while working, and he was only thirteen at the time. Abuela was lucky to get a job working as a maid, and the woman she worked for encouraged her to keep educating herself whenever she could, giving her books to read. That was also where she met Abuelo, who was visiting the people she worked for. He fell in love with her and insisted she marry him. Although he took good care of her, she never stopped worrying that it would all disappear, or someone would die unexpectedly."

Jonah chewed, a thoughtful expression on his face. But after he swallowed, he didn't comment. Rob wasn't sure whether it was his habitual reticence or something else causing him to not say whatever it was on his mind, and he didn't feel secure enough to ask.

Things were still pretty tenuous between them, in every way.

The moon was rising above the horizon by the time they were finished eating, not full but waxing—a lopsided disc casting silvery light on the water. There was something so peaceful about the scene that Rob exhaled, losing much of the tension tightening his shoulders.

"It's beautiful here," he said. "Now I understand why people rave about the Low Country."

"As beautiful as some of the other places you've been?"

There was both curiosity and a hint of wistfulness in his tone.

"Most places have some particular beauty," Rob replied. "But not every place will speak to my soul the way this one does." It was difficult to find the right words, but he felt as though he needed to try. "From the first moment I drove into town, I knew it was going to become a special place to me."

Jonah chuckled. "You're a romantic."

"Is that an accusation?"

Jonah's eyes were twinkling. "Maybe…"

Rob shook his head in pretend sadness. "Well,

I am one, and proud of it. I feel sorry for you if you're not one too."

"I'm a realist," Jonah shot back, grinning. "Practical to a fault, or so I've been told. Aunt Lonie tells me so all the time."

"Hmm… But don't you think your dream to sell everything and travel the world is even a little bit romantic?"

That seemed to surprise Jonah, whose eyebrows lifted. A thoughtful expression crossed his face, and his gaze grew distant.

Finally, he replied, "Not really romantic. It's not like I plan to just drift around. I want to visit other places to broaden my mind and knowledge base. There are some things you can only learn by experiencing them."

"So, you're viewing it as an intellectual exercise, rather than an adventure?"

Jonah turned in his seat, so as to face Rob completely. The gleam in his eyes had morphed from amusement to something Rob thought almost fanatical.

"Every other member of my family has traveled extensively or lived in other places. It was something my grandmother, and her father's family, believed in, implicitly. My great-grandfather made his money at sea and explored much of South America. My grandmother traveled all over Europe and parts of Africa and Asia before she married, and sent both her daughters to school abroad—Mom in France and Aunt Lonie in Switzerland. Lonie stayed afterward to travel and learn from famous chefs before coming home. Even Carmen spent a lot of her childhood in New Orleans with her father's family, and then went to France to study. After school she spent a few years working as a chef on private yachts, sailing all over the world.

"I'm like the country cousin, you know? The local yokel, stuck here stagnating, with no experience of the world at all."

Shocked and moved, Rob just stared at him for a moment.

"You've got to be kidding," he finally said. "You don't really feel that way, do you?"

Jonah shrugged, looking away to try to catch the waiter's eye. "Maybe."

"But intellectually you must know that isn't true? That just because you're not as well traveled as some others in your family you're somehow not as good?"

Ignoring the question, Jonah signaled to the waiter for the bill.

"Seriously." Rob persisted, wanting to get to the truth. "You don't think that, do you?"

"No, of course not." Jonah's lips twisted, and

he shook his head for good measure. "You make it sound far more intense than it really is. I just want to live a more rounded, interesting life. That's not such a bad ambition, is it?"

"No, it's not." But even as he agreed, and while he was wrangling with Jonah over who would pick up the tab, Rob realized he didn't believe the other man's protestation. Instead, it was as though Jonah's dream was somehow born from a sense of inferiority, rather than desire.

And that knowledge made him incredibly sad.

Jonah left the restaurant feeling like a fool.

He never spoke about such intimate thoughts with anyone. What was it about Rob that made him spill his guts in that way, opening himself up to ridicule?

Clearly Rob thought he was nuts, and Jonah was inclined to agree with him—nuts for having said anything.

They crossed the parking lot in silence, then got into his vehicle without exchanging a word. Rob had a thoughtful expression on his face, and Jonah couldn't help worrying that he was reconsidering…well…everything.

They were driving out of the parking lot before Rob spoke.

"Where are you going to go first?" he asked suddenly, jolting Jonah out of his thoughts.

"What?" he asked, wondering if he'd missed part of the conversation.

"When you start traveling. Where are you going to go first? You must have an idea?"

He didn't know why, but Rob's seemingly honest interest lightened his mood.

"I have a friend from college who's involved with a group that travels to various countries to help organizations that work with endangered species. She's sure she can get me at the very least an interview to join them."

"You'll be a shoo-in." Rob's voice held conviction. "With the work you've done, they'll be salivating to have you."

"I wish I had your confidence," he said, then snapped his mouth shut. Rob really did bring out the honesty in him, and it was disconcerting.

"You should. You have a stellar reputation, a winning personality, and you're damn gorgeous to boot. Who wouldn't want you on their team?"

Jonah was so surprised, he couldn't stop himself from laughing out loud, so hard and long he had to dash tears from his eyes.

"What?" Rob asked. "You don't believe me?"

"Not one word of it," he agreed. "Although I like that you think I'm gorgeous."

"You knew that already," was the sanguine reply.

"Did I?"

"If you didn't, you should've."

Jonah snorted, not knowing what to say to that. He wasn't used to being complimented. Not about his looks anyway.

"What kinds of animals are your favorites?"

The change of subject almost gave him whiplash.

"Sorry, what?"

"What types of animals are your favorite? I'm partial to mammals myself. Never could really get into reptiles, although I treat them when I have to."

Amused by that pronouncement, Jonah was tempted to tell Rob he loved reptiles, but there was something about the other man that demanded honesty.

"Ungulates," he replied. "I've always been fascinated by them."

"You mean horses, in particular?"

"Nope. Cattle, pigs, camels, llamas, alpacas—you name it."

"Interesting…"

He glanced at Rob and found him leaning

against the passenger door, gaze trained on Jonah's face. He quickly looked back at the road so as not to get mesmerized by those piercing eyes.

"What's so interesting about that?"

"I'm not sure," Rob said, a hint of laughter in his voice. "I'll need to think about it. I was brought up on a cattle ranch, and the first thing you learn is not to get attached to the steers, so I have a hard time feeling close to cows. I like alpacas and llamas though."

"Have you ever treated one?"

"Nope. Not yet."

Jonah put on his indicator to turn into his driveway. "Then a word to the wise—they can kick sideways, like camels."

"Good to know," Rob said, laughter warm in his voice.

Jonah drove around to the back and used the automatic opener to gain access to the garage. Suddenly nervous, ready to jump out of his skin, he turned to face Rob after turning off his vehicle.

"You'll come in?"

"If you want me to. No pressure."

"None from me, either," he replied, the words wanting to stick in his throat.

"I definitely want to," Rob replied, his tone

like warm molasses on a sultry summer day. "But would it sound weird to say I'm nervous?"

And, just like that, Jonah knew it would be okay.

"I am too," he admitted. "But let's see where things go. Come on. I have to take Eunice for a walk, so that'll take some of the edge off. Nothing like a ramble with an elderly dog to show you how to take things slow."

Rob was laughing softly as he got out of the vehicle, and Jonah couldn't resist joining in.

Once inside, they were greeted by Eunice, who looked expectantly between Jonah and the back door.

"Hang on there, sweetheart," Jonah said, before turning to ask Rob, "Do you want a beer?"

"I probably shouldn't, since I still have to get myself back to the hotel. One's my limit when I'm driving."

Without thinking about it, Jonah replied, "Have it, if you want to. There's plenty of space here. I can definitely find room for you."

*Preferably in my bed.*

He didn't say it aloud, but perhaps his expression gave him away, because Rob's eyes flared bronze and hot, and Jonah found himself having to look away.

The intensity of desire he felt when Rob

looked at him that way was almost frightening, and he was suddenly unsure of how to deal with it.

But he was determined to find out.

# CHAPTER THIRTEEN

ROB COULDN'T HELP noticing the aura of suspense and anticipation that surrounded them as Jonah popped the caps on two beers, handing him one, before opening the door to let Eunice out. They followed the golden down the stairs and into the warm, fragrant night at her leisurely pace, walking shoulder to shoulder, brushing against each other with each step. The moon was higher in the sky now, shedding silver light across the plants, creating secretive shadows beneath the trees.

He vaguely noticed the manicured lawn and flower beds, along with the rich scent of still-damp grass, more in tune with Jonah's movements and breathing than his surroundings. Jonah lifted the beer to his mouth, and Rob found himself mirroring the movement, even while thinking how badly he wanted to replace the bottle with his own lips.

He'd been craving a taste of Jonah since the first instant he'd seen him again, and as Eunice snuffled around the base of a hydrangea bush, he knew he didn't want to wait a moment longer.

They'd both stopped walking, and Rob turned to face Jonah, staring at his profile for an instant. His heart was hammering, his body tightened with need, and he swallowed before saying, "Suddenly the thought of kissing you in the moonlight is the most important thing in the world."

Jonah froze, and Rob saw him take a deep breath.

Without moving, Jonah asked, "What are you waiting for, then?"

Rob shifted to stand in front of the other man, so he could look into those sexy eyes, which gleamed beneath their sleepy lids.

"Permission," he replied, so softly the word seemed to disappear into the night.

Jonah stepped closer, so their bodies were just a fraction of an inch apart, and Rob could feel his warmth reaching out to him, and he trembled.

"You have it," Jonah said, equally softly, and Rob rejoiced to hear the tremor in that rumble of words.

But now that the moment was there, Rob found himself wanting to savor it—not rush, although his body clamored for him to do so.

Using his free hand, he stroked across one of Jonah's eyebrows, along his cheek, to the corner of that beautifully shaped mouth. Learning the contours of his face, relishing the sensation of warm skin, the slight abrasion of facial hair beneath his fingertips.

Jonah was almost preternaturally still beneath Rob's questing fingers, only the rush of his breath giving an indication of his excitement.

Then, as Rob watched, he licked his bottom lip.

The wave of need that crashed through him made Rob unable to wait a second more, and, cupping the other man's cheek, tilting his head, he bent to cover that luscious mouth with his own.

At the first touch of lips, soft and a little tentative—exploratory—they both groaned, releasing a groundswell of desire that had shimmered just below the surface. Rob inhaled, taking Jonah's scent deep into his lungs, his head swimming with the sheer glory of this first intimacy.

Jonah's arm went around his waist, pulling him near; tightening to tug him even closer yet, if that were possible, and Rob wanted to absorb the other man into himself.

Or be totally absorbed by him.

Tongues tangled and danced together, arms

encircled, and there was no mistaking the arousal they shared in equal measure. Rob tilted his hips, rubbing his erection against Jonah's, and the carnality of the sounds that emerged to be lost in each other's mouths was unmistakable.

The sensations threatened to overwhelm him, and Rob broke away. At least fractionally. They were still in each other's arms, but he resisted the draw of Jonah's mouth to rest his forehead against the other man's.

And just that contact still felt right.

"Kiss me again," Jonah growled, his body straining toward Rob's. "Or bring those lips back here so I can kiss you."

How could he resist such a demand?

But when their lips met again, it was with a sort of barely restrained ferocity that threatened to break the chains of his control, and Rob gentled the kiss incrementally, giving himself a chance to regroup as best he could. Sweeping his lips back and forth against Jonah's, he teased the other man before abruptly dropping his mouth to Jonah's neck to lick and suck.

The response was electric. Jonah arched, his head going back, his pelvis tilting forward, his arms tightening so he was hanging on to Rob, as though afraid if he let go, he'd fall.

*There.*

*That spot.*

Jonah was shivering, harsh sounds of arousal breaking from his throat, and Rob wanted more. Much more than was achievable in a garden in the middle of the night.

Moving his mouth up to the other man's ear, he growled, "I think we should go inside soon." Swirling his tongue along the edge of Jonah's ear achieved another groan of acquiescence and pushed Rob's desire even higher. "Before I make love to you out here."

"Yes."

It was a deep rasp, and an acknowledgment of mutual need. But Jonah didn't let go, his arms still tight around Rob, his body shivering and straining. Somehow, in that moment, Rob knew not just how badly he wanted Jonah, but also recognized the intensity of emotion building within.

That he wanted not just to make love with him, but show him how much he valued this time together. How much he valued Jonah, just the way he was.

And how much he wanted to give him pleasure—physically, emotionally, mentally.

Any way he could.

Loosening his grip, but putting his arm around Jonah's waist, he turned them back toward the house, calling to Eunice over his shoulder. As though realizing the men weren't really paying her much attention, the golden snorted but obediently trudged along behind them.

They broke apart to go through the door, Jonah waiting for the dog to make her entrance, while Rob took the two almost untouched beers and put them on the counter. Eunice made a beeline for her bed in the corner of the kitchen, and, silently, Jonah walked through to a small staircase at one side of the room and began to climb.

Rob followed, hearing the sound of their footsteps echoing through the enclosed space, slower than his racing heartbeat, as he stared at the broad back and tight ass of the man ahead. The climb felt monumental—not because the staircase was long, but because Rob knew, without a doubt, that his life would never be the same again, once they'd reached the top.

Taking the last two steps in one stride, he caught hold of Jonah's arm just as the other man turned the corner on the landing above. When those dark eyes widened in surprise, and Rob saw they were glazed with desire, he dragged Jonah close to kiss him again, and felt Jonah's body melt into his.

Without conscious thought, he pressed Jonah against the wall, pinning him there, kissing him over and over. Tugging at Jonah's shirt, he freed it from his pants, so as to plunge his hands beneath, letting his fingers race up his taut abs, along his ribs and across the wide chest, finding the tight nipples and lightly pinching.

Jonah was hanging on around Rob's neck, his fingers plunged into Rob's hair, keeping him in place as they kissed and kissed and kissed, breathing into each other with gasps of air and quiet groans. Whereas before Rob had wanted to rush straight to a bedroom, now *this* was all he wanted.

The sensation of mouth on mouth, Jonah's hot satin skin beneath his palms, the sounds of desire stretching out into the darkened corridor.

Then, just as suddenly, it wasn't enough.

Forcing his lips away from Jonah's felt almost impossible, but he somehow achieved it to ask, "Which way?"

Jonah was slow to answer, as though he had to bring himself back to the present to be able to reply, "First room on the left."

Taking his hand, Rob moved swiftly that way, tugging Jonah along behind him.

Jonah stumbled in Rob's wake, his legs weak with desire, his entire body one erotically charged nerve ending. Holding on to Rob's hand provided the only stability he had left to him, so he clutched it tighter.

He'd never been kissed that way before—with such intense mastery—or felt such a rush of desire while being kissed. He could still taste Rob on his tongue, feel the hard length of his body pressed to his, held the scent of him—skin and breath—in his nostrils, and those lingering sensations made him feel high.

If just a few kisses and caresses made him lose himself so completely, what would making love with Rob do to him?

A trickle of fear invaded his brain, but as they entered his bedroom, and Rob searched for then flicked on the light, it floated away.

Rob's eyes were dark, his face tight, his lips—so sinful—were puffy from their kisses, and the sight of him drove Jonah to a new level of lust.

Letting go of his hand, Rob took three steps into the room, then turned to face Jonah, who still stood just inside the doorway, too weak and addled to move.

"Come here."

Rob spoke softly, almost tenderly, but there was an edge of command in the words too, and Jonah's body reacted as though touched.

There was no thought of refusal. No hesitation.

He walked slowly forward, his gaze caught on Rob's. Snagged like a fish firmly on the hook.

"Undress for me," Rob said, still in that soft tone, but making it more of a demand than a request.

Tremors fired along Jonah's spine, and his hands were shaking, but again he didn't hesitate. Something about the situation, the night, made whatever might happen completely right.

Deep inside he knew, with utmost certainty, if he balked at anything Rob wouldn't try to force him into it, and that level of trust was beyond price.

He didn't know just how he was so sure of that, but he was.

Taking off his clothes took only a few moments, and when he straightened from removing his pants and underwear, he froze, transfixed by the expression on Rob's face.

"Damn," Rob groaned. "You're so gorgeous."

Jonah stared in disbelief, and it must have shown on his expression, because Rob stalked closer, slowly, intentionally.

"You don't think I'm telling the truth," he stated, keeping Jonah's gaze captured with his own.

All Jonah could manage was a single shake of his head.

"I'll show you that I mean it," Rob said, and the conviction in his tone made Jonah tremble even more.

Rob pulled off his shirt, then toed off his boots as he was unzipping his jeans. It was torture to watch and wait, but absolutely thrilling at the same time. When Rob was naked, he pulled back his hair and started to secure it at his nape with an elastic band.

"No." Jonah found his voice then. "Leave it loose. Please."

The look Rob sent him was incendiary, as he slipped the band back onto his wrist and said, "For you, anything."

Before Jonah could respond, Rob was right there, pulling him close. And as their bodies collided, all coherent thought left Jonah's brain.

Rob was kissing him, and they were moving in what seemed almost like a slow, inexorable dance toward the bed, before falling together onto it, mouths still locked in kiss after kiss.

Then Rob lifted his head and said, "Let me show you I meant what I said."

Starting at Jonah's head and working his way down, he proceeded to do just that, searching out all the most sensitive erogenous zones, some of which Jonah didn't even know he possessed. Losing all sense of time and space, his world contracting until all that remained were the two of them, and the sublime ecstasy Rob propelled them toward.

All vestiges of control vanished, ceded to Rob in a way Jonah, in the dim recesses of his mind, realized he'd always wanted but had never been able to do with anyone else.

Rob demanded his complete and utter surrender, guiding him into a whole new world of sensual delights, keeping him on the edge of release for what seemed like eons, holding him there effortlessly. In freeing himself from his need to be in charge, losing himself in Rob's concentrated focus and command, Jonah soared to heights of bliss he'd never experienced before.

When his first orgasm crashed through him, he heard himself cry out and, burying his face in a pillow, almost wept with satiation and relief, as Rob found his own release almost simultaneously. Feeling, for the first time in too long to remember, that he was, in that moment, absolutely enough.

# CHAPTER FOURTEEN

JONAH WOKE UP the next morning alone in bed, but with the memory of Rob grumbling as he got up to leave in the wee hours of the morning. When he'd sleepily suggested the other man just stay the night, Rob sat down on the side of the bed to put on his boots and shook his head.

"Small towns, man. Your reputation is probably already in jeopardy as it is. Let me at least try to mitigate the fallout by sneaking back into the hotel before anyone's on the road."

It had been on the tip of his tongue to say he didn't care, and that thought was scary enough to keep him silent.

He'd protected himself—his life and desires—from the people around him for so long, the knowledge that he was already willing to throw that away after just one night in Rob's arms was shocking.

So, after a long, sweet kiss that made him want to drag Rob back upstairs, he'd let the other man out and stumbled back to bed, too exhausted to do anything but savor his lingering satisfaction before falling deeply asleep.

Now though, with sunlight trickling into his room, wide awake and with no distractions, it was time to put the sex aside—as difficult as that may be—and seriously consider the ramifications of last night.

It had been amazing. If he were a romantic like Rob, he'd even go so far as to say it had been magical. But he had to remember it wasn't the start of something more. Neither of them, he believed, were destined to remain for any length of time in Butler's Run, and the trajectories of their lives were completely different.

Sooner, rather than later, they'd part ways, and Jonah couldn't afford to get so tangled up with the other man that he'd be hurt. Silly then to feel an ache around his heart at the thought of no longer having Rob in his life.

And remembering the way he'd allowed Rob to take the reins in bed, he had to wonder whether that new power dynamic would threaten to spill over into other parts of their lives. If Rob would feel emboldened to try to boss him around at work.

That thought brought him up and out of bed, scowling, to go take Eunice for her morning walk. It would be a problem he'd face head-on if it came up.

But that eventuality, at least, didn't come to pass.

When he got to work, his stone face firmly in place and determined not to treat Rob any differently than he had before they'd ended up in bed together, it was refreshing to have Rob clearly on the same page.

"Morning," he said, when he strode into the clinic, smiling and sending the greeting out to everyone in general. "What's on the agenda today, boss?"

That was directed to Jonah, but in such a casual way no one would imagine that just a few hours before they'd been rolling around naked together.

"Saturdays are short days," he said, striving for the same sanguinity Rob was displaying, but having to battle with himself to achieve it. Hard to sound unconcerned when his heart was pounding and memories of the night before wanted to flood his head. "We close at three, but we're usually flooded with patients. Mostly pets owned by folks who work and find the weekend the best time to have appointments. Plus, with closing yesterday because of the power outage, we might have to squeeze a few of those patients in too. Inez asked for the day off to go spend some time with her family, since she knew you'd be here, so you'll be running your own exam room today again."

"Sounds good," came the reply, and Rob went off to check on Milo and Ovaltine before getting his room set up, leaving Jonah wishing he'd sent him even some small acknowledgment of what they'd shared. A sly smile maybe, or a wink.

Then he caught himself up, feeling a little silly at his own contrariness.

The day flew by, filled with mostly run-of-the-mill patients, and before he knew it, it was time to clean up the clinic and head home.

Rob came by the office after his last patient, knocking lightly on the open door, standing just inside the room.

"Do you need me for anything?" he asked.

Now, there was a loaded question if ever he'd heard one, and Jonah had to hold back a snort of amusement.

"No, I think everything here is good to go," he replied, trying to keep a straight face.

Rob's eyes darkened, and Jonah's amusement faded. Clearly the other man had heard the subtle subtext behind his words and he too was thinking about all the things Jonah wanted—needed—from Rob.

"Are you sure?"

The words, and even the tone, were innocuous, but his expression, visible only to Jonah and not the staff members passing back and forth in the corridor, was not.

It sent a tsunami of desire through Jonah's body, so intense that he couldn't break free from Rob's gaze, even if he'd wanted to. And he shook his head, since to say no aloud was out of the question.

"Okay," Rob said, as though Jonah had nodded. "See you later."

When he backed out of the room, Jonah was so surprised he almost called him back, but didn't.

The encounter left him flustered and confused, not knowing how to interpret it, but only a minute later his phone pinged, and it was a text from Rob.

Can I take you for dinner later?

Come by the house. I'll cook.

I'd ask if your cooking is as good as your aunt's, but it doesn't really matter. I'm not that interested in food anyway. Not when you're around.

Thankful that no one could see his face, Jonah spun his chair around, just in case, as he could still hear voices from the rear of the clinic. He was instantly aflame on reading Rob's words.

Hopefully we'll get around to food at some point. Come by in about an hour. Park by the garage and come to the kitchen door.

Putting the phone down after receiving a thumbs-up from Rob, Jonah leaned his head back against the chair and contemplated the ceiling, trying to figure out exactly what he'd gotten himself into.

It felt crazy, this rush of desire, the need. The speed at which they were going didn't faze him, simply because in the past he'd slept with men the same night as meeting them. But he'd never felt as connected to any of them, and he certainly hadn't craved them afterward.

In reality, he'd often felt somehow diminished by the encounters—sad, a bit depressed and lonelier then than before.

He'd been trying to scratch a sexual itch when he'd gone off to Atlanta to the clubs, not looking for someone special or a relationship. What did he know about relationships anyway? His mother had never married again after Daddy's death, and his grandmother had also been a widow. Aunt Lonie's marriage hadn't lasted more than a few years too, before she divorced

Carmen's father and he went back to New Orleans. All the most important people in his life had been alone. Independent. Seemingly unwilling to get back into a couple situation. To Jonah, that spoke volumes.

It also left him with a gap in his emotional education. You can't really know how to be if you haven't seen it in practice, can you?

Then he shook his head and tried to put all of those thoughts out of his head for the simple reason that he wasn't really in a relationship with Rob, and never would be.

Two months, Beeta had said, before Rob got bored and tired of Butler's Run and went somewhere else.

In his mind, the word relationship implied commitment. Long-term.

Whatever this was between him and Rob, it wouldn't last, so there was no use worrying about it.

And he might as well enjoy the thrill, to the max.

The question he asked himself now was: what would be the best way to do that?

Rob got back to his hotel room and took a long, hot shower before heading back to Jonah's, trying to work the kinks out of some sore muscles.

But he didn't mind the discomfort, not in the slightest. Especially when he remembered how he'd got it.

He groaned under his breath and stuck his head under the water, but that didn't erase the images his memory conjured up.

Jonah had been so responsive, so receptive to Rob's attentions, it had blown him away. He couldn't remember ever feeling the way he had last night—so completely into the man he was with that nothing else mattered.

Sure, he'd been telling the truth when he told Jonah his greatest pleasure came from giving pleasure to whomever he was with, but last night had gone way beyond that.

There'd been no way to know what Jonah would or wouldn't like, and Rob had gone strictly on instinct. And somehow—by fate or serendipity again—he'd gotten it totally right.

Not just for Jonah, but for himself too.

His easygoing nature and bone-deep desire to make others happy hadn't really given him the opportunity to determine exactly what gave him the ultimate pleasure. He'd always simply taken his cues from the men he'd been with, and been happy enough with that. But with Jonah he'd found his true sexual self, and the result had been explosive.

Mind-blowing.

He'd been a bit worried after he'd left that Jonah would revert to the reticence of before—going back to keeping him at a distance. After all, although he'd known the other man had enjoyed the lovemaking, Jonah had been clear about his habit of seeking out one-night stands and no-strings-attached couplings. He'd also been adamant about keeping his private affairs out of Butler's Run. The combination of those two factors had kept Rob wondering if their first time together would also be their last.

Now he knew that wasn't the case and was thrilled.

Jonah's determination to leave Butler's Run wasn't something he wanted to think about. Not now, with the memories of the night before swirling in his head, arousing and elating.

Instead, he'd concentrate on relishing every moment he could with Jonah, while making plans and preparations for the future.

For the first time in years, he felt at peace with himself and his life, and he wouldn't allow doubts or fears to dull the joy.

Quickly finishing his shower, he rushed to dress, picking out the most casual clothes he had, and making the decision to go online and order some plain T-shirts, casually comfortable pants and shirts. It was freeing to know he could once more dress the way he wanted, and not have to worry at all about his Vet Vic persona ever again.

The relief was palpable.

He had to remind himself not to speed while driving to Jonah's. The urgency he'd felt when deciding whether to tell Jonah he was attracted to him hadn't abated, just morphed into something different—the desperate need to be with the other man as much as possible.

Before Jonah took off to live the life of adventure he'd always wanted.

Driving around to the back of the house, as Jonah had directed, it struck him that doing so meant no one would see his vehicle if they came up the driveway. He understood, of course, but knowing the risk Jonah was taking even by having him here added to his underlying tension.

When he knocked on the back door, Jonah called for him to come in over Eunice's barks, but when Rob opened the door, he saw the golden still lying in her bed, quiet now, but with her tail going a mile a minute.

"Some guard dog," he said with a chuckle. "Didn't even bother to get up."

Jonah laughed. "Eunice knows when to exert

herself, and that's only when absolutely necessary."

He was standing by the sink, peeling potatoes, dressed in a loose pair of running shorts and a form-fitting T-shirt, looking so delectable Rob forewent his usual greeting to Eunice. Instead, going straight to Jonah, Rob encircled his waist from behind, bending to kiss the dip just below his ear. Jonah shivered and made a sweet, rough sound in his throat.

"If you keep doing that, you won't get any food tonight," he said in that delicious rough growl his voice became when he was turned on.

Rob pressed closer and murmured into his ear, "You're all the sustenance I need right now. We can always order in."

Jonah shivered again, the potato peeler going lax in his hand. But he made no further protest when Rob insisted they go upstairs.

Later in the evening they finally made it back downstairs to the kitchen and set about cooking together. Rob finished peeling the potatoes while Jonah snapped some beans, after taking the steaks he'd seasoned previously out of the fridge.

As they worked, they talked about a variety

of subjects, working their way back to Rob's potential purchase of the clinic.

"I know it'll take a while to figure out the details, if you decide to sell after all," he said, putting the potatoes into the pot Jonah had given him. Setting it on the stove and turning on the burner, he continued, "And in the meantime, I'm going to start looking for an apartment or small house to rent. The hotel is fine, but not an economically sensible choice, over time. I figured the best way to go about it would be to contact a local realtor. You know one?"

Jonah was quiet for so long, Rob wondered if he'd heard the question, but before he could repeat it, Jonah said quietly, "I think you should move in here."

Stunned, Rob asked, "What?"

"You should move in here, with me." There was no nuance in his tone, nothing to indicate why he was suggesting it. "There's plenty of room. In fact, there's an almost self-contained suite upstairs you could have, which would give you space and privacy."

Still shocked, needing a moment to think, Rob went to the fridge and took out a beer. When he held it up, silently asking if Jonah wanted one as well, the other man nodded. Then, in unison, they both headed to the back door and out onto the porch, Eunice following them.

As the dog made her ponderous way down the steps into the garden, Rob and Jonah sat side by side on the porch glider and each took a sip of beer, as though postponing the upcoming conversation.

In reality, Rob was just trying to wrap his head around what Jonah had suggested. While part of him was absolutely ready to agree to the arrangement, the more cautious part of his nature wanted more information.

"You can say no," Jonah said. "Without hurting my feelings. It's just a suggestion."

"I don't want to say no," Rob confessed. "I just need to understand why you'd be willing to do that."

Jonah snorted. "Is it that preposterous an idea?"

"No. It makes sense on a lot of levels, except one that I can think of."

"Which is?"

"You've made it clear you don't want people knowing about your private life. Even if everyone thinks you're putting me up as a friend, or because you want the rent money, or whatever, eventually there'll be talk. Doesn't that bother you?"

Jonah shook his head. "Maybe you have the wrong idea about me. I'm not in the closet. The entire town knows I'm gay, and has known for years. What I didn't want is people seeing the way I was living—the hookups and such. I'm sure anyone with half a brain and any interest in the subject would guess I was getting me some somewhere, but there was no evidence of it here, which is what I cared about.

"With you, it's different. I won't care if they think you and I are involved."

Rob's heart leaped, excitement and a strange type of hope unfurling in his chest. But he wouldn't—couldn't—allow it to take root.

Wouldn't let himself think that what they had might make Jonah change his mind about leaving. Might make him want to stay.

But he couldn't help it, and that kernel of optimism allowed him to say, "Okay, then. I'll move in…here."

And it was his need to protect his heart that made him hesitate, and say it that way, instead of what he'd really wanted to.

*I'll move in with you.*

# CHAPTER FIFTEEN

THE MONTH FOLLOWING Jonah's invitation to Rob to move in seemed to fly by, and Jonah couldn't believe how happy he was, or that it could last. Even his long-held belief that leaving Butler's Run to see the world was what he needed to do seemed to fade into insignificance when he was with Rob.

It never failed to amaze him—the closeness they'd come to share. Although they both worked and lived together, there was little conflict, and Jonah never tired of being around the other man. They just fit.

Yet, there was a part of him that constantly watched, waiting for the first signs of boredom in Rob. Not even the fact that Rob went out and bought a pickup truck, saying, "I figured I'd need something like this for the rougher farm roads," made Jonah believe he would stay.

Trucks could be sold as easily as they were bought.

Two or three months, Beeta had said, and Jonah had no reason to believe Rob's sister would be wrong.

Which was why whenever Rob asked if he'd contacted the lawyer about the legal paperwork, he kept putting him off. He also made sure to involve Rob in all the farm, livestock and sanctuary visits, making sure he knew what he'd have to do if he stayed. They were invariably messy, sometimes backbreaking, and often futile—like when they spectacularly failed to corner the pig that needed its hooves trimmed, and it took off, busting through a fence to escape.

Jonah had to admit that Rob seemed to take it all in his stride; he even seemed to enjoy himself.

How long that would last was anyone's guess.

In the moments when he allowed himself to think about it, Jonah realized all he wanted was to keep things the way they were until it was over, as he knew it eventually would be. He refused to even contemplate the state of his own heart, which he suspected had given itself, completely, to Rob.

When that thought crept into his head, he reminded himself that he'd survived without the other man in his life, and he could do it again, when necessary.

Nothing lasts forever, as his mother had always said, especially in reference to her husband and the marriage Jonah knew had made her so very happy. Happy enough that no other man ever stood a chance with her, after her husband died.

"My parents got married when they found out Mom was pregnant with me," he told Rob one night, when they were lying in bed together, entwined, talking about their families. "Daddy left college and joined the army, and Mom finished her degree a couple years later. Mom always talked about how they'd planned to travel after college—join an organization like the Peace Corps—and see the world. Daddy was studying to be an engineer, and Mom was studying toward a degree in education, so they'd be a good fit for something like that. She always sounded so wistful when she spoke about it."

Rob was silent for a moment, his long, gentle fingers tracing up and down Jonah's arm, soothing now, rather than arousing, the way they often were.

"So you think they gave up that plan because of you?"

"I know they did. If I hadn't come along, they could have followed their dreams, and maybe..."

He'd never said it out loud before—that secret pain and guilt he felt—and couldn't get the words out now.

"And maybe your father wouldn't have died when he did?"

Jonah froze, the air suspended in his chest to hear his greatest fear spoken out loud in that way. It took an instant to regain his equilibrium, and his first instinct was to deny that was what he'd been thinking.

But, as always, Rob had a way of pulling the truth right out of Jonah's heart.

"Yeah," he admitted softly. "Yeah. I've always wondered..."

"Aww, babe."

Just those softly spoken words and the way Rob tightened his grip, as if to shield Jonah from the hurt, was enough to dull the long-agonizing suspicion. And he appreciated the fact the other man didn't try to tell him it was stupid to hang on to those feelings, which first arose when he was a child, but simply acknowledged his right to have them. Even if, intellectually, they made no sense.

Rob had that effect on him too—making him bring long-hidden emotions out into the open and question them also. Something about Rob's steadying presence brought all kinds of old stories and feelings bubbling to the surface to be examined and somehow mitigated.

There was consolation in the fact that he wasn't the only one opening up.

One evening, sitting on the porch, watching Eunice nose around in the garden, Rob said, "I heard from Beeta today. She's trying to convince me to do another documentary. This one down in Costa Rica."

Jonah's heart sank. *Here it comes.*

Swallowing against the dryness in his throat, he asked, "What did you say?"

Rob shrugged. "I told her no, although it was hard to do. She knows family is my weakness, and always tries to exploit that."

"You said you felt bad because she didn't get the support from your parents when she wanted to go to college, so you helped her. It seems a little...unfair...that she's still pressuring you, when you said you don't want to do the videos anymore."

What he'd really wanted to say was that Beeta was being downright selfish, but he didn't think it was his place.

Rob sent him a sideways glance, his lips lifting in a rueful smile.

"I love her, but I'm not blind. The truth is, Beeta always wanted to get her way, immediately, and had a wicked temper. Abuela never knew how to deal with her, other than to give her whatever she wanted, which made my parents angry when they found out, and then she'd get punished. So, on one hand Beeta was spoiled, and on the other she was almost constantly in trouble. As her older brother, being closest in age, I felt as though I had to help, somehow. Protect her." He shrugged, and his smile was sad. "Long ago I realized it made me easily manipulated by her, but I didn't have the impetus to make it stop. I do now though."

Jonah wanted to ask what had made the difference, but the words stuck in his throat. Stupid to think maybe it had something to do with their relationship—or whatever the heck to call what they were involved in.

"I'm proud of you," he said, and meant it. "Breaking out of old habits is hard."

Rob smiled, his face lighting up in a way that always made Jonah's heart sing. And when he leaned over for a kiss, there was a sweetness to the meeting of their lips that had little to do with sex, and everything to do with emotion.

And it was almost too much for Jonah to bear.

Rob couldn't remember a time when he'd been happier, or more on edge. The longer he stayed in Butler's Run, and with Jonah, the more confident he became that this was where he belonged. And Jonah, even more than the town, was the reason. Yet, although he thought he and Jonah were perfect for each other, there was a sensation of distance between them sometimes too.

A watchfulness on Jonah's part, that gave Rob pause.

But he didn't know how to broach the subject, or what to do to allay whatever lingering fears the other man had.

He desperately wanted to prove to Jonah that they belonged together but knew it was a fool's errand. The more they spoke about Jonah's family and his past, the easier it was to see why he was desperate to escape his small town and live a life he considered more fulfilling.

It would be easy to point out just how important he was to the town he wanted to leave. Tell him how far he'd come, and how much everyone admired and appreciated him, but Rob knew it wouldn't make any difference.

Just as admitting his love for Jonah wouldn't change anything.

And why should it? Just because he knew what he felt was love, didn't mean it gave him the right to make demands, no matter how much he wanted to.

In bed, he was in charge. In life, they both had to do what was best for themselves, irrespective of whether one or the other of them was going to get hurt.

Best to make the most of the present happiness, right?

Now, if he could just get himself to believe that and put all his trepidation aside.

He had better luck integrating himself into the life of the town, which seemed quite happy to accept him. Sure, there were one or two people who made a point to be unpleasant, but that happened everywhere, and it didn't faze him one bit. What did annoy him were the people who insisted on calling him Vet Vic. That part of his life was well and truly over, but convincing everyone of that fact clearly would take some time.

"What can you expect?" Jonah asked, obviously trying not to laugh at Rob's annoyance after another encounter with the pink-haired Emma Gorman, who not only refused to use his real name, but constantly asked when next he'd be filming. "Obviously she's angling to be featured in your next documentary."

Rob rolled his eyes. "As if that'll happen."

"Which one? The documentary, or Emma being in it?"

"Both," he said, trying to put a snap in his voice but failing in the face of Jonah's amusement.

"But when we went to her farm, you obviously fell for the alpacas. Don't you wanna film them?"

"Now you're just being a brat. Remember how Donny spat in my face?"

They both dissolved into laughter, which was something they did so often, it was hard to remember how solemn Jonah had seemed at first. Even at work he seemed more relaxed, despite the brisk workload. The clinic was thriving, making Rob wonder how he'd be able to keep up, should Jonah decide he was ready to sell.

But that was a topic Jonah seemed unwilling to discuss at any length. Each time Rob asked what the lawyer had said, Jonah had some excuse about why he hadn't contacted her, and Rob let it go. After all, when the paperwork was actually prepared, it would mean the beginning of the end for them as a couple, and Rob didn't want to think about that.

One thing he could say though was that Jonah made sure to show him the full extent of what being a country vet entailed. While Rob was well-versed in dealing with cattle and horses from growing up on the ranch, working with some of the other animals was something he hadn't done since vet school.

Pigs, he discovered, whether pets or farm animals, were especially challenging.

"I dealt with a few potbellied pigs back in LA," he told Jonah. "But never one of that size."

Since Rob happened to be sitting in a mudhole, and the animal in question was halfway across the adjacent field with the owner and Samantha the vet tech chasing after it, Jonah didn't seem inclined to answer.

Or maybe it was because he was laughing too hard. So hard, in fact, that he had to prop himself up on a nearby post to stay on his feet.

Obviously Rob still had a lot to learn, like how to properly use a piece of board to corral a pig in the corner of a pen without getting flattened when the pig broke free.

But he was reveling in all of it.

He hadn't had many doubts about staying in Butler's Run, and with each passing day his decision was confirmed.

This was where he belonged.

The only thing that would make it more perfect was if Jonah and he were planning to build this life together, but Rob accepted that wasn't meant to be. He'd gotten to know Jonah better, recognized the deep-seated need the other man had to venture out into the world. To explore and learn and grow in a way he didn't think he could in his hometown.

Perhaps to live out the life he felt his parents had been deprived of.

It was more than just a dream, and Rob doubted Jonah would ever be truly happy if he didn't experience the life he'd been hoping for all these years. If he were to stay and become bitter and discontented, Rob would be heartbroken.

And more than anything else, he wanted Jonah to be happy.

# CHAPTER SIXTEEN

THEY SETTLED INTO a routine of sorts. Work, of course, and making love every night, but Rob also insisted that Jonah show him around the surrounding area, so, on Sundays, they would drive to various places. Hilton Head, Charleston, Savannah, Augusta and the environs. Jonah found himself seeing places he'd known all his life in a whole new way as he absorbed Rob's genuine enjoyment. Whether walking through a historic district, swimming in the ocean or exploring a nature preserve, Rob's natural curiosity made every trip a fun, learning experience. And it didn't matter if they ate at a diner or a five-star restaurant, went to a roadside carnival or aquarium, Rob's cheerful charm turned it into an experience.

They were driving home after one of their jaunts, Jonah at the wheel, singing along to the radio, when his phone rang and he answered it through his vehicle's hands-free capability.

"Cassie," he said, letting his pleasure at hearing from his old friend show in his voice. "Happy to hear from you. Are you back in the States?"

"I am," she replied. "For a short time anyway. I'm hoping to have time to see you. I'll be in Philly for a couple of weeks, then I don't know."

"Maybe I'll take a day off and meet you halfway, unless you want to fly down to Charleston? I want to hear all about your time in Tanzania."

"I'll let you know," she replied. "But either of those would work. We definitely need to catch up. It's been too long. But, in the meantime, I wanted to tell you that the hiring freeze has been lifted, and the organization is taking applications again."

From the corner of his eye, he saw Rob shift in his seat, but Jonah didn't dare look over at him.

"Mmm," he said, his brain churning, not sure how to react.

"I know it's short notice, but it literally just happened. And you said to let you know when it happened. They have some exciting opportunities coming up, including a potential posting in Borneo, and another in Zimbabwe. I think you'd be perfect for either of them."

"Thanks for letting me know," he said, wondering why he felt not one iota of excitement at hearing the news, after champing at the bit for years. "Give me a call when you know how long you'll be here, and whether you have time for us to meet up, okay?"

"Okay," Cassie said, a note of surprised confusion in her voice. No doubt she'd been expecting a far more enthusiastic response to her news, since the hiring freeze had been in effect since the start of the pandemic. "I'll call you again during the week. Get your résumé in order."

"Thanks again. Bye."

The silence in the vehicle after he'd hung up seemed heavy, especially after the fun atmosphere from before. Jonah wasn't sure what to say, if anything, and eventually it was Rob who spoke first.

"Is that your friend who works with the international organization you want to join?"

"Yeah. She's been in Tanzania for over a year, but she got permission to come back for Mom's funeral. Cassie spent a lot of time with us during holidays and such. She lost her parents in an accident when she was young, and Mom never liked the idea of her spending vacations on her own, so she extended an open-ended invitation to her."

Aware he was babbling, he closed his mouth

and kept his eyes on the road, although he really wanted to see Rob's expression.

"Your mom sounds like a really nice lady."

"She was."

He almost added that he wished Rob could have met her, but that sounded somehow too intimate for this particular conversation. So when Rob lapsed into silence and busied himself with apparently trying to find another station to listen to on the radio, Jonah followed suit and shut up too.

When they got home, Rob said he was going to have a shower and went upstairs without inviting Jonah to join him. Just as well, since Jonah felt the need for a little time to himself to think about Cassie's call and what he should do about it. Letting Eunice out into the back garden, he grabbed a bottle of water and went to sit on the porch where he could watch her poke around.

This was an opportunity to follow his dream, finally. Cassie always had the most interesting stories about her travels, not just about the animals and work, but about the local communities too. With the longer postings, sometimes up to two or three years, there was the chance to integrate into the societies she worked with. That was something Jonah found so attractive about the organization she worked for. They believed those long postings created better cooperation between their employees and the people they were assisting and training.

In the past, whenever he thought about getting a two-year job in Africa or Asia or South America, excitement had churned in his belly. Now, though, he felt…

Nothing.

No thrill.

No enthusiasm.

Nothing.

But that wasn't completely true either.

There was a definite emotion building in his chest, and he struggled to ignore it, not wanting to give it a name. No avoiding it though.

It was sadness.

How had things changed so much in such a short period of time?

It was Rob, of course. The way he made Jonah feel. How he'd made life so much brighter and more fun-filled.

How he'd caused Jonah to fall in love with him, and forget everything else that had been so important. Turned his life upside down.

It made him a little angry, and very confused, and he wondered how things would change now. He didn't want things to change. Everything had been…well…perfect over the last couple of months.

Except they'd had the knowledge that their relationship wouldn't last hanging over them. One or the other of them would leave. Maybe both would—going on with their lives alone.

Now that the moment was on them, Jonah was no longer sure of what he wanted for the future.

No, he knew what he wanted.

Rob.

But he wasn't sure the other man wanted him the same way, and he wasn't sure he was strong enough to ask.

Jonah heard Rob coming down the stairs into the kitchen and braced himself, dreading the conversation to come, although he knew it had to happen.

He heard the fridge open and close, then the creak of the screen door as Rob came out onto the porch. Although he was tempted to look at the other man, he kept his gaze trained out into the garden, where Eunice had found a patch of sunlight and settled down to snooze.

"We need to talk." Rob sounded determined, as if he was expecting Jonah to brush him off.

"I know."

The other man exhaled audibly.

"I know that call came out of the blue, and

maybe you don't feel ready to apply, but I think you should."

And Jonah thought his heart had just shriveled and died.

Rob watched Jonah's profile, noting that the other man was stone-faced. So different from the smiling, laughing companion of just an hour or so ago.

Not that he blamed him. It was a painful situation, and he couldn't wrong Jonah for wanting to keep his emotions to himself.

Rob wished he had the same ability, because right now he felt as though he wanted to fall apart and wasn't sure he could hide the agony eating away at him. Yet, he knew he owed it to Jonah not to add more stress to the situation by revealing how hard all this was to him. After all, it wasn't Jonah's fault Rob was in love with him.

"I'm not sure it's the right time," Jonah said, his voice low but steady. "There's the clinic to think about, and Eunice too."

"You know I want to buy the clinic. I haven't changed my mind about that. In fact, I want it more than ever. And I'll take care of Eunice for you. That's not a problem."

"You have it all worked out, huh?"

There was a hint of bitterness in Jonah's

tone—or was it hurt? Whatever it was released Rob from the constraints he'd placed on himself, and he knew he had to be completely honest. Even if it meant embarrassing himself.

"No. I don't have it all worked out. This is killing me."

Jonah stiffened, then slowly turned in his seat to face Rob, and the stony mien cracked, ever so slightly. Just enough to give Rob some solace.

"I love you," he said, before Jonah could say anything. "Do you know that I came here to Butler's Run because I saw your name on the proposal the Marsh Tacky people sent to Beeta?" He wanted to get up and pace, energy and fear crackling beneath his skin, but he forced himself to stay where he was, holding Jonah's gaze. "I had a crush on you in college, but by the time I worked up the courage to tell you, you were gone. And since being here with you, I've never been happier.

"If I had my way, you'd stay here with me, forever. But this is too important for you. It's a dream you've had since you were a child, and if you don't take advantage of this opportunity, you'll regret it forever. Maybe become bitter about it. I couldn't stand that."

Jonah was staring at him, eyes not sleepy anymore, but wide with what looked like shock.

"You love me?"

His deep, gravelly tone sent electricity along Rob's spine, but he wouldn't allow himself to hope.

"Yeah, I do. But you can't take that into consideration. I won't let you. You need to think only about what you need to do, to be happy. We can work out the details, whatever they turn out to be, but you have to follow your dream."

"My dream." Jonah said it almost like a question, and then fell silent, his gaze locked on Rob's.

"Yes. That's what's important now."

"No." Jonah shook his head.

"No?"

Instead of elaborating, Jonah stood up and held out his hand to Rob.

"No. What's important right now is that I love you too, and we're here, together. Everything else can wait."

His heart missed a beat, as Jonah's admission rocketed through him like a strike of lightning. And he didn't have the strength to resist when Jonah led him inside and up to their bedroom.

They'd work it out later, he thought, as they came together with a ferocity that not only showed their feelings, but was tinged with desperation.

Waking up later, Rob found himself alone in bed and, rolling free of the tangled sheets, pulled on a pair of shorts and went downstairs in search of Jonah. It was still light out, summer sunshine lingering later and later into the night.

Jonah was at the kitchen table, his laptop open in front of him, an expression of concentration on his face.

"Whatcha doin'?" Rob asked, before yawning his way over to the fridge for a water. Then it struck him that Jonah might be applying to the agency, and his stomach knotted. But he made it a point to cross to the table and kiss the top of Jonah's head, to make sure he knew whatever was to come, Rob was on his side.

"I'm looking at various agency websites," he said. "To see what's available, either for short-term projects or on a volunteer basis."

Knees suddenly weak, Rob plopped down into a chair and stared across at the other man.

"Why?"

"Because you're right. I do want to see more of the world than this little corner, and the way I dreamed of doing it feels right to me, still. What no longer feels right is the thought of leaving Butler's Run and all I've built here forever, especially if I can keep building it with you."

Unsure he was actually hearing him correctly,

Rob shook his head, not in negation, but in confusion.

"I don't understand," he said.

Jonah smiled, his eyes gleaming.

"I thought, if I can find an organization that does short trips for vets to various countries, I could do a trip or two a year. You could run the clinic, and we could get a locum if we need to for while I'm gone, but then I'd be here for most of the time in between." He hesitated for a moment, his gaze sharpening. "If you're in agreement, that is."

The easiest way to answer him was to get up, drag Jonah to his feet and kiss him silly, saying, "Yes, yes, yes," in between each deep, love-filled kiss.

He'd been given a second chance with Jonah Beaumont, and he was grabbing hold of it, with both hands.

And never letting go.

# EPILOGUE

ROB SLUNG THE duffel bag onto the back seat of his double cab and slammed the door shut. Then he turned to Jonah and pulled him close, burying his face into the other man's neck for an instant. But because they were in the pickup zone at the airport and it was chaos around them, he let him go quickly, before a cop came to hurry them along.

"Get in," he said, after one last squeeze. "And let's go home."

"Yes," Jonah answered, pulling open the passenger door, relief and love swirling through him in equal parts. "I can hardly wait."

Once Rob had pulled out into the stream of traffic heading away from the airport, he shot Jonah a sideways glance. Jonah watched the other man's profile, drinking it in, unable to tear his gaze away, even if he'd wanted to. Which he didn't.

"That was the longest six weeks of my life,"

Rob said, checking his mirrors before changing lanes.

"Mine too," Jonah admitted. "Rwanda was amazing, and I learned so much, but damn, I missed you terribly. The next time they ask me to do more than three weeks or a month, tops, I'm saying no."

"Praise the Lord and pass the gravy," Rob replied, which made Jonah sputter with laughter.

"You've been hanging out with Aunt Lonie again, haven't you? She's the only person I know who uses that expression."

"Auntie and Carmen kept me so well fed, I think I put on ten pounds since you were gone. Even if I hadn't been stress eating most of the time, I'd still have been unable to resist their food."

They'd kept in touch as best they could, mostly through email and the occasional video call when Jonah was back at base, so he already knew there'd been some issues with the locum they'd hired to fill in while he was gone.

"How bad was Mitchell, really?" he asked.

"He could have been worse," Rob replied. "But not by much, when it came to customer service. Apparently, he thought working in Butler's Run was the equivalent to being in the middle of nowhere, and everyone there was a total idiot. I had to do some fancy footwork not to lose any clients, and I only saved a couple because I promised them he wouldn't be around for long and that I'd look after their animals myself if necessary."

"Emma Gorman?"

It was Rob's turn to laugh. "How'd you know?"

"Wild guess."

Which made them both snicker, in perfect synchronicity.

When they got home, Jonah got out of the truck and stretched, looking around at the house and garden, smiling. He was home, and he couldn't be happier.

Rob had already retrieved Jonah's bag, and he slung his free arm around Jonah's waist, tugging him close.

"Welcome home, love." Rob sounded as elated as Jonah felt, and they walked side by side up the porch steps, only separating so as to be able to unlock the door.

It was sad not to have Eunice there to greet them, but she'd passed away, peacefully in her sleep, the year before. Instead, it was Rob's two dogs, Skipper and Mary-Ann, that were jumping and prancing around the kitchen, back ends waggling as hard as possible.

Rob dropped the duffel on the floor and

turned to yank Jonah into his arms to kiss him, as though he'd never stop.

They'd been together for more than two years, and the love and passion between them never waned. Of course, now it was heightened by their time apart, but Jonah knew that was incidental.

When he was with Rob, he knew he was home.

And that was more than enough.

\* \* \* \* \*

*If you enjoyed this story,
check out these other great reads from
Ann McIntosh*

The Vet's Caribbean Fling
The Nurse's Holiday Swap
Twin Babies to Reunite Them
Christmas Miracle on Their Doorstep

*All available now!*

# HARLEQUIN
### Reader Service

# Enjoyed your book?

Try the perfect subscription for Romance readers and get more great books like this delivered right to your door.

See why over 10+ million readers have tried Harlequin Reader Service.

**Start with a Free Welcome Collection with free books and a gift—valued over $20.**

Choose any series in print or ebook. See website for details and order today:

## TryReaderService.com/subscriptions